P9-DIA-173

LINCOLN CHRISTIAN COLLEGE AND SEMINARY

growing in authority relinquishing control

A NEW APPROACH TO FAITHFUL LEADERSHIP

celia allison hahn

Research from The Alban Institute

The Publications Program of The Alban Institute is assisted by a grant from Trinity Church, New York.

Copyright 1994 by The Alban Institute, Inc. All rights reserved.

This material may not be photocopied or reproduced in any way without written permission.

Library of Congress Catalog Card Number 93-74586
ISBN 1-56699-125-0

CONTENTS

88520

ACKNOWLEDGMENTS

My grateful thanks to all who have served as my teachers in this project:

—The sixteen interviewees whose honest revelations about their struggles to exercise authority faithfully made them my primary teachers;

—Colleagues who read all or part of the draft and generously provided me with essential critique: James R. Adams, Donna Schaper, Dorothy Lee, Speed Leas, Susan Blackburn Heath, Douglas A. Walrath, Loren B. Mead, Barry Evans, Edward A. White; and other colleagues who provided advice about the design of the research (noted in the Appendix);

—David McClelland, an important teacher for me, whose book *Power: The Inner Experience* suggested key concepts for integrating the interviewees' accounts with developmental theory;

—Learners and co-teachers in courses on authority at St. Mark's Church, Toronto School of Theology, Alban Institute courses, and other groups;

—Teachers in institutions—members and colleagues in The Alban Institute, the functional education program at St. Mark's Church, the Shalem Institute for Spiritual Formation;

—My spiritual mentor, in whose roomy presence I have experienced all these things: loving support for becoming confident that I am loved by God, affirmation for experiments with Assertive authority, the courage and clarity to discover how I take inappropriate control, a model of Integrated authority responsive and flexible enough to turn on a dime.

CHAPTER I

What is authority? and Where do you get it?

We need a new look at authority!

Keith Mason, Solicitor General of New South Wales, Australia, struggles daily with the exercise of his authority at work, at home, and in the church. When the commissioners on the Law Reform Commission consistently turned in their reports late, Keith experimented with various responses. His efforts to speak with them directly ended in frustration. Setting an encouraging example was gentle but ineffective. When he took over the tasks himself he knew he was coopting their responsibility and when he complained about the commissioners to others he felt dishonest.

The issue about authority doesn't go away when Keith returns home from work. "I can't get my five-year-old to go get into the bath when it's time for the bath," he complains. Life with a five-year-old seems to require sudden switches in role—from loving friend to stern authority figure. Sometimes the question—at work or home—seems to come down to "Look, who's in charge?" But Keith is clear that's not what is really at stake.

The question about what kind of authority he has and what to do with it comes up at church, too. As a committed layman, Keith Mason is convinced that "the lay person is the voice of what the real church is all about." But the church offers him no authority; in fact he finds himself engaged in a long-term struggle to press an unwilling church to ordain women as priests. Keith Mason's authoritative positions—as Solicitor General of New South Wales, as father, and as a leader in the Movement for the Ordination of Women—give him no easy answers.

Halfway across the world, Davida Crabtree, minister of the Colchester Federated Church in Connecticut, finds both joy and struggle as she seeks to exercise her authority as a parish pastor. "Dee," as most people call her, finds her chief joy at those moments when everything comes together, when she can say, "My experience of God in the midst of that process is within the community and within my own process... [which] I experience as a very deeply spiritual one." It's a "whole person experience...like stepping into a warm shower."

In the parish, Dee tries to help church members "discover the authority of their own lives." "I try to enable the group to claim *its* authority," she says. She works hard "at not using power in a way that is over against but instead...in a way that empowers." Out of those convictions about authority, Dee tried to find ways to introduce the ministry of the laity as a central theme "in such a way that it would fit...with their understanding and could then begin to stretch them."

In her effort to encourage shared authority, the joy of "everything coming together" is accompanied by dilemmas about how to make authority truly mutual. When it seemed that the church needed to move to two services on Sunday, Dee didn't want to say "I'm making the decision." When resistance arose, how could she best manage the process? After the whole church voted not to invest in companies doing business with South Africa, and she discovered that the committee in charge had secured the services of an investment firm that adhered only to the Sullivan principles, how could Dee translate her convictions about authority into responsible decisions? How could she support the duly appointed committee chair while at the same time honoring the vote of the congregation and her own conscience? How would she work through the conflict and misunderstanding toward an outcome where "we" are responsible—not just "me"?

Years ago, as one of a small minority of ordained women, Dee remembers that "my authority was challenged every single time I opened my mouth." Though her confidence helped her stand firm, today that confidence still gets tested. Dee recalls a recent encounter on a search committee, when a powerful male member expressed negative opinions about a candidate Dee considered qualified. She was tempted to make an end of the matter in her own mind by concluding, "Oh, well, of course he knows what he's talking about." Then she struggled to marshall the "discipline in myself to bring myself to speak up in that situation, where my view is different."

Keith Mason and Dee Crabtree describe experiences and dilemmas that are familiar to me, and probably to you, as well. How can I be true to myself, serious about my responsibility for a project, without trying to control other people—or just giving up and hovering ineffectively on the sidelines? How can I deal with resistant parishioners or irresponsible staff members? How can I be open to others while remaining faithful to my own deeply held convictions? Both Dee and Keith face situations where their concern to hold their authority faithfully and effectively seems to call for mutually contradictory actions.

How many lay people like Keith find that the church denies them any authority? How many clergy want to use their authority in an empowering way but find themselves stymied or embroiled in conflict?

And what of those graced moments when God's call and presence, my own truest self, the freedom and energy of the others, and the responsibility and blessedness of the community—all play together as in a great symphony? Have you wondered what makes those shining moments happen? Can we find a way to be more open to them, to learn not to get in the way of their happening? And can we know God is in the process without claiming that knowledge in a way that turns our authority into authoritarianism?

In sum, how are we to hold our authority?

Throughout our churches I see men and women, clergy and laity wrestling with this question. The word "authority" signals an elusive reality: every time we try to close our hands on it, it escapes in a different direction. "Legitimate power" is a conventional and serviceable definition to begin with, and we will be enriching it as we proceed in this exploration. But even after we define the word, "authority" sounds abstract. If we stop to think for a moment, however, each of us can recall a vivid, personal history with parents, schoolteachers, police, "authorities" in church and state—a history that arouses in us strong and ambiguous feelings—longings, disappointments, admiration, anxieties. If we continue to push past the seeming abstraction of that word "authority" and ask thoughtful people like Keith Mason and Dee Crabtree a few prodding questions, we will uncover moving, fascinating, and useful stories about the crucial authority issues they are facing in their work and ministry right now.

Many members of churches on the more "liberal" side of the ecclesiastical spectrum are seeking to discover an authority different from the brand claimed by fundamentalist churches. Like Dee, we want the courage to "speak up" and the openness and skill to work toward decisions that are "ours" not "mine." We want, in other words, to be authoritative, but not authoritarian. We want to proclaim our faith boldly without denying that mystery pervades our lives. But what is that different vision for which we long? Does authority mean something different from "getting my way"? Like Keith, we may come to the uncomfortable realization that proving "I'm in charge" misses the point. Is authority more than "enablement"? In our confusion many of us find ourselves flipping between two cherished goals that often seem to conflict: we want to take charge and lead courageously, and we want to engage with others in a mutual, collegial way.

Uncertainty within breeds difficult encounters with others. Clergy and laity often seem anxious and critical as they eye each other's authority. Clergy face new dilemmas about their own authority. The traditional consensus about pastoral authority has collapsed. In the shadow of ecclesiastical academics and bureaucrats, parish pastors often feel they have little authority. On the margin of society, shrinking in numbers, churches themselves wonder what authority they can claim. New wisdom from the human sciences keeps challenging our traditional understanding of what it means to be a leader. As clergy wrestle with their own authority, they are increasingly aware of the central importance of lay people's ministry in the world. Laity face their own dilemmas. Urged to own their ministries at work, at home, and in their communities, they are simultaneously given the message Keith hears, that clergy, not laity, are the real authorities.

Both men and women have new questions about their own authority. Women are reaching beyond passivity; men are seeking authority that is more than control. Dee, a confident woman, must still marshall the discipline to express her opinion when it differs from that expressed by authoritative males. Both men and women show new signs of a concern to exercise their authority in the light, not only of their own experience, but that of the other. Keith finds his primary experience of "church" with women denied ordination. Looking across all these boundaries, many people are beginning to sense that the church is a whole, a system, and that they can't solve their own problems in isolation from the others.

Some church people cherish a vague and mournful sense that people *used* to have an authority that has slipped into the past and become lost.

Or somebody *else* may exercise authority, not me. Most of the people I've interviewed began with a protest: "Until you told me that I'm supposed to be a person who exercises authority, it was not something that I was conscious of doing." These words came from Keith Mason. If *anybody* can claim authority, we might expect a Solicitor General to do so!

Our limited view of authority as "something other people have" may point to one root of our difficulties. Approaches to questions of authority in a Christian context have been primarily objective and institutional—denominations' justifications of their own authority structures or theories about how various kinds of leaders affect groups. Insufficient attention has been paid to the *inner* dilemmas people encounter when they struggle to exercise authority within a Christian context—dilemmas like the one we've heard Keith and Dee wrestling with: "How can I exercise my authority in a way that helps other people claim *their* authority?"

I could not find resources that met this practical need of clergy and laity, women and men, to grow in their own authority. The books I could find, helpful as they are, talk about *other* people's authority, and offer no direct help in meeting the challenges we face in exercising our own.

In summary, we in the church today are deeply concerned about how to live with authority; our understanding of it is fuzzy and contradictory; and we get little practical and personal help from those who talk about it in objective, institutional terms. As I wrestled with those difficulties, I began to see that we might find a way out of our confusion about authority by shifting our perspective: becoming curious about our own inner experience of authority, probing our struggles and joys as people who exercise authority every day, and reclaiming the church's own special search for how the gospel story illuminates our inner and corporate life.

The Study

When she wanted to learn about dying, Elisabeth Kubler-Ross asked dying people themselves about their experience. I decided to follow a similar approach in exploring authority. Instead of standing outside theorizing, I would ask the insiders, clergy and lay ministers, about their own experiences with authority. I became convinced that our best sources for new clarity lie in two places:

—the practical wisdom of clergy and laity, men and women, who are discovering effective ways to tackle the dilemmas about authority in their own lives

—the gospels' picture of Jesus, who spoke with an authority that consistently transcended passivity and control.

I decided to limit my inquiry to the local congregation and the primary actors in that setting: parish clergy who work to equip laity for their ministries and lay people who move out from the congregation in a conscious effort to exercise their ministry at home, in the workplace, and in their communities. Confining the study to parish clergy and laity promised a clear focus close to daily life where the local church meets the world. I interviewed sixteen people in all: equal numbers of parish clergy and lay people, of men and women.

Since I was about to embark on a sabbatical to New Zealand and Australia, I would have an opportunity to look beyond the particularities of U.S. culture and include a more varied group of religious traditions. Interviewees thus included Anglicans, Uniting Church in Australia (which joins Methodists, Presbyterians, and Congregationalists), in addition to members of the United Church of Christ, Episcopal, American Baptist, and Presbyterian churches. The group included one African-American and one New Zealand Maori.

Interviews formed the first source for the inquiry; the second source was a study of the picture of authority in the gospels. Third was a search of all the "authorities" on authority I could lay my hands on.

This book is based primarily on the first two sources—practical experience and sacred lore—with special attention to the moments of discovery where those two kinds of truth intersect. I hope you accept my invitation to join the research study, pausing to explore those "intersections" in your own life through the periodic reflection sections designed to assist readers in examining their own experiences of authority and discovering their growing edges.

What is authority?

Before you read on, I suggest you find pencil and paper (or, even better, a friend, especially if you are an extravert) and spend a few minutes answering this question: "What is authority, in your experience?" Then

you will have a better chance of adopting an authoritative stance toward the responses of others.

Interviewees acknowledged that they have authority partly because it's *recognized* by other people; as one put it, "...the reason I know I have it is because other people tell me." Maoris "always look to the priest," said Howard Ashby, New Zealand Anglican priest. "They expect a priest to be on the marae [the Maori sacred place] if anybody dies. They look to the priest for guidance..."

Most of the men and women, clergy and laity, with whom I spoke, however, wanted to emphasize that they saw authority as an *inner* reality. Authority is "to know from the inside who you are," said one. Jim Adams, Rector of St. Mark's Church, Capitol Hill, in Washington said:

> For me, my authority is my capacity to be what I consider authentic: saying what I really think and feel... That's where authority resides rather than with titles, roles, and positions... When I hear my colleagues who are in trouble with their congregations start talking about *their authority as the Priest and the Rector,* I know they are in trouble.

These comments echo the New Testament emphasis on *internal* authority. We constantly encounter Jesus defining himself ("I am...") and rejecting other people's authority to take over that task, as when he deftly sidesteps the trap laid in Luke 20:2: "Tell us by what authority you do these things, or who it is that gave you this authority."

Authority also means *to act... to speak:* Authority is "the permission and/or obligation to act"; it's "the ability to get things done"; it's "your voice." In the Bible, authority is expressed in action. One meaning of *exousia* is "the ability to perform an action."[1] Psalm 33 speaks succinctly of God's authority: "He spoke and it was done."

Authority is *recognized, it comes from within,* it means *to act;* authority is all of those, and it is linked to the transcendent dimension of life. For Dee Crabtree it's very simple: "God called me to ministry." Listen to Ruth Shinn's way of describing this "more than." She is a Division Chief at the U.S. Department of Labor and a UCC laywoman.

> I think of authority in two ways: one in the global or religious context... There's a structure in the universe. I feel called toward

love and justice. The other kind of authority that I recognize: I think human beings create nations or institutions. They make compacts with each other, and within those compacts they establish rules. [Sometimes you have to] challenge one kind of authority because you feel the compelling force of the call for justice, [though you don't do that casually].

In the Bible we hear constant echoes of that same sense of the conjunction between the cosmic and the conventional Dee and Ruth are describing.

So interviewees said authority is *recognized, inner*, it means *to act... to speak*; authority is all of those things and points beyond them toward God.

Are their responses like yours, or different in some ways?

"Where do you get authority?" I asked

Take some time to think about your own answer to this question before reading what other people said. Where do you experience *your authority coming from?*

Here are the interviewees' responses.

1. Authority is *given*, and therefore *received*. They saw the givenness of authority, first of all, in their growing-up experiences. Childhood experiences held many kinds of gifts. Many mentioned the gift of affirmation: "Fairly early in life, I got the message that I was okay, that I could be secure in who I am." Many had experiences that conveyed the message, "You can do it." Some recounted experiences of testing, or encouragement to think for oneself. Family messages were important. Peter Sherer, who raises millions of dollars for AIDS, said: "My family...gave me a sense very early that I was a Sherer and that we had work to do in the world." Both family and school conveyed the message that "the responsibility was to identify and then use your God-given talent..."

They experienced that other people gave them authority. "People used to tell me their life stories," remembered Dorothy McMahon, minister of the Pitt Street Uniting Church in Sydney.

I'd get on trains and they would tell me their life stories, and I'd get on buses and they would tell me their life stories, and I would sit in my mother's [living] room and they would tell me about themselves. As I went on...I began to be open to the possibility that if people were prepared to trust me with themselves, maybe there was some gift I had; maybe people felt in some way safe in telling me things. I regarded that as a sort of sacred trust, but also as a certain authority to take up my ministry.

Clergy, of course, found that their congregations gave them authority to take up their ministry. "You get it when they give you the keys," said one young pastor. Dwight Lundgren, American Baptist minister in Providence, Rhode Island, said, "You've been hired to do a certain job...; people are expecting you to make sure things operate in a certain kind of way... And so there is the authority that they just give to you..."

And some said their authority was given them by God. I asked Howard Ashby, Anglican Maori priest in New Zealand, "Where do you get your authority?" He replied, "From God. And the people." The gospels, too, are very clear that authority is God-given. The Father gives authority to the Son. We see Jesus continually giving authority away. The disciples hear the message: You teach; you heal; you forgive—do the things that are the prerogative of God, as Jesus did. And they invite others into that authority.

2. Where do you get authority? You get it *from within*, said interviewees. Several pointed to the way early experiences, received as gifts, later became inner realities: "I've had a sense that I am a person of worth ever since I was little. That authority is now within me." Many were insistent that "It's not just because I was given this role." "It didn't just happen because I was in this slot." Colin Bradford, international economist, said, "The way I like to be judged is on the basis of what I've said or written or think, not because I happen to be from Yale." Dwight Lundgren, the Baptist minister who said he'd been hired to do a job, also explained that authority comes from "having a sense that I'm comfortable with myself and understand the limits of who I am and what I do, and that who I am is not co-terminous with my role as a minister. And that allows them to be who they are also...Even if I weren't being paid to do this, I'd be sitting here wondering about God, thinking about these things and talking to people about them."

Authority comes from the experience of God within. Dorothy
McMahon spoke of "that inner authority in myself which is of God..."
(though she is wary of making an unambiguous claim to that authority).
In the gospels, too, authority is based on direct experience, from within.
The authority of the apostle is: "I have seen the Lord."

3. Authority is given. It comes from within. Third, *"I take it,"* said
respondents. Assertiveness is a key ingredient in "authorizing" experiences, as Dwight Lundgren's story illustrates.

> I remember vividly, I was a teenager... It was Laymen's Sunday,
> and my father had been invited to be one of the three men who
> would speak. And suddenly it dawned on him halfway through the
> week that he also had a business appointment and had to be out of
> town. So I am sitting there... as he calls whoever is in charge of the
> service and says, "I can't do this." And...I just said, "That's all
> right, *I'll do it."* And I was sixteen... So that was the first time I got
> up and spoke in church, and the minister and a lot of people came up
> afterward and said, "This is what you ought to be doing."

Joyce Yarrow, who is President of the Institute for Non-Profit Training and Development in Hartford, says: Yes, you are given authority,
but also "you must take the authority; you must assert your own authority." She acknowledges that even when "what I have to say is most
important... it may not be heard and listened to by the group, but *I take
strength in myself and make that happen."*

4. Authority is given. It comes from within. You take it. But
there's more. People say authority comes *from many sources integrated,
and they say it comes from God.* Many of them find it difficult to distinguish the source: it's a meeting of person, context, initiative, and the
transcendent. Verna Dozier, lay teacher, consultant, and author, describes the integration this way: "I certainly do feel that it's a gift, that
it's a gift that I claim. So to that extent it comes from within me. And
it's a gift that's affirmed by the community, so in that way it comes from
other people."

Davida Foy Crabtree described the blended ingredients of authority
from the perspective of a parish pastor:

> It's like there is a discernment process that I go through in which I
> am factoring in a great deal of data, both sensory data and intuitive

data... and then [using] my mind to think through what's best, and by that process my authority is not a contravening authority but is instead an integrative authority for the people I am working with... [That deeply spiritual process is] somehow integrating within me all of what's happening around. Yet at the same time it's not least common denominator politics...It's a leadership oriented integration of all the information that I can figure out about the situation. And I use my authority as little as possible...I try to enable the group to claim *its* authority...My experience of God in the midst of that process is within the community and within my own process.

Dee Crabtree's experience illustrates well the "person-in-context" quality of Integrated authority: the inner and outer dimensions flow together instead of contradicting each other. For her, as for others, this wholeness points to God: "For me there was never any question about where I get my authority. God called me to ministry. That's my source of authority." That's the source of authority for biblical people, too. For them, authority belongs essentially to God, who gives it away in a manifold delegation. Time after time the gospels picture Jesus giving authority away to the disciples as though it were an abundant commodity. The point was emphatically *not* to get busy arguing about which followers could exercise authority over the others. "It shall not be so among you." Those who hold Integrated authority know that they hold it as a gift— only in partial, broken ways, to be sure—but also in the awareness that it is a gift for the community, not a personal possession to be employed for their own benefit.

The interviews echo the gospels, too, in their clarity that people can act with authority in situations where they can't get their own way. This concern to distinguish authority from control was dramatized in a story about Nelson Mandela some time ago:

Visitors to Mandela in prison noticed a curious authority that the prisoner seemed to exert over his warders. When they escorted him, he set the pace. One visiting lawyer remembered how Mandela marched briskly into the visiting room at the prison accompanied by four warders one day and said, "George, I'd like you to meet my guard of honor." He then courteously introduced the warders.[2]

So people say *authority is given, it comes from inside you, you take*

it, and it comes from all those sources. It comes from God. A group of
United Methodist clergy with whom I worked came up with this summary:

> Received authority: "It should be done."
> Autonomous authority: "I'll do it my way."
> Assertive authority: "Do it."
> Integrated authority: "Let's do it."

In the next chapter we will look at how people seem to experience those
four sources of authority as they move through their lives. Because I
believe that an inquiry like this one must acknowledge not only the usefulness of conceptual schemes but the chaos of real life, I will attempt to
do both. Chapter 2 develops the theory about patterns of growth in
authority. Chapter 3 explores four practical dilemmas in the exercise of
authority from a perspective close to the disorder and pain that usually
characterize our adventures in leadership. Chapter 4 traces men's and
women's journeys through the four stages of growth. Chapter 5 moves
back to *stories* of laity and clergy, beginning with the "messy" quality of
real life and only then noticing how the theory emerges in those stories.
Chapter 6 moves beyond individual experience to reflect on what it
means to live corporately in Integrated authority, with the help of three
biblical metaphors for the church—a colony of heaven, the body of
Christ, and the church as Servant. At many points, questions for your
reflection are included, which may be easily adapted as designs for a
study group.

Participate in the Interview Process

*Most interviewees reported that pondering these questions for an hour
gave them important new clarity about their authority. Therefore, to
claim your authority, to make this exploration your own and derive the
most benefit from it, don't just read the book! Participate in the interview process in the way that seems most promising to you. You might
use the interview questions in the Appendix A (see page 187) for a
journal-writing exercise. You could find an equally curious partner and
take turns interviewing each other, taping the interviews or taking notes
for each other. You could also use the interview questions to guide a
series of discussions in a support group.*

CHAPTER II

Patterns of Growth in Authority

There is no roadmap to Integrated authority. Each of us discovers markers on a trail that is ours alone, with all its false starts, backtracking, skirting of precipices, suddenly discovered mountain passes. Looking back, we see a path marked by singularity embraced in providence. No roadmaps have been charted; but if we examine our own and others' growth in authority, we can discern some sequences noticed by solitary travelers, philosophers, and developmental theorists.

People often begin their stories with accounts of Received authority: the gifts of childhood experiences, the authority "laid on" at the beginning of a pastorate or other job. "You get it when they give you the keys," said one pastor. Experiences of Received authority were often followed by the discovery of Autonomous authority. Women especially remembered that discovery as an "aha," a significant turn in the road. Loma Balfour, Anglican priest in New Zealand, tells this story:

> I was just following along for a couple of years behind my husband [a long-time priest]... I've spent quite a lot of the last eighteen months, which is how long I've been in the parish, just trying to get a grip on what it is to be a vicar for *me*, and to some extent to try and unload the strong modelling which I've had from my husband... and find my own way... There's been a few fireworks. [He will say,] "Oh, you should just do this, Loma," and at first I fell into the trap of trying to do it like that and not being able to do it, and then he'd give me heaps for not doing it properly. I've got to the place now where I can say, "Look, darling, it's no use. I'm not you, and I can't do it that way." So we're progressing. [With church officials she perceives as putting down women,] I'm certainly a long, long

way down the track now. I can just eyeball them and say, "Just cut it out."

Men's ahas tended to be different. Many of them had discovered the limitations of Assertive authority and were moving beyond it. Glenn Farquhar-Nicol, a young minister of the Word in the Uniting Church in Australia, reflected on his new approach:

> At first I think my sermons were like a big stick: here's a vision of the gospel—get cracking. I've changed. I've had to acknowledge that others had visions that were at least as legitimate. A top-down attitude doesn't get anywhere... There's another way our vision can be realized: by beginning where people are, encouraging them, awakening their hopes. It's a gentle process, recognizing them as people, a mutual process... My early authoritarian view was not positive. It's better to get alongside people, nurture and nourish them. I changed from a dragging mode to an encouraging mode.

Women tell stories of liberation from passivity; men tell stories of liberation from control. The tendencies differ, but the sequences are congruent.

Philosophers have speculated about those sequences for centuries. Hegel posited a movement from thesis to antithesis to synthesis. Tillich saw people moving from heteronomy (the law of others) through autonomy (the law of self) to theonomy (the law of God).

Throughout life we discover ourselves in the tension between our need to say "I'm me" and our need to say "I'm with you," between our desire to receive and our desire to act. In the struggle to find our balance and move forward, we tack back and forth like sailboats trying to make progress in the face of prevailing winds. Early on we shift from dependence on other people's authority to the discovery of our own, from being receivers toward becoming actors. But after separating, we often come home to the realization that we will reach the fullness of growth not by abandoning the gifts we began with, but by adding to them. And so we begin to contemplate the possibility of holding together what we had seen as opposites, surrendering our reactive independence ("Nobody's handing anything to me!") and moving from an "either-or" posture toward a paradoxical posture. Growing in our willingness to inhabit a widening world, we progress from "my authority" to "shared authority grounded in God."

We can discern these sequences not only in the grand sweeps of Hegel and Tillich, but also in recent developmental theories, where we observe the progression from a heteronomous ("conformist," "conventional") starting point, to an autonomous ("individualistic," "post-conventional," "subjective") protest, on to an assertive posture characterized by "initiative," and then to an integrated position characterized by "integrity," universality, paradox, and "generativity."[1] I am particularly grateful for David McClelland's work on stages of development in power described in *Power: The Inner Experience*,[2] to which the following discussion owes a great deal.

There's no roadmap, but there are some paths. Let's trace these well-worn sequences as we pick our way along the trail.

1. Received Authority

Our first experience of authority is that "other people have it, and I don't"; for many, this state of affairs persists throughout adulthood. Richard Tustian, Presbyterian layman, a retired land use planner, said,

> I tend to think of...other people's authority and how I would relate to that... As a layman you don't exercise any authority in the church, do you?... I've been Clerk of Session. I guess there's supposed to be some authority goes with that position, but there really isn't any... I just don't perceive myself as being put in an authoritative position in the church. In fact...it runs the other way around. The clergy is the authoritative person.

This layman finds himself on the receiving end of other people's authority in his church life (I don't think that is true in other arenas of his life).

People may then progress from a posture of responding to other people's authority to receiving their own, ready made. A few interviewees' authority comes already shaped in roles they receive, rather than actively define and shape. Howard Ashby, the New Zealand Maori, spoke consistently of the priest's role as traditionally defined by his people: "The people always said to me, We put you there and we pull the strings. They can ring up at all hours, and they say, We want you to come. So-and-so is very sick, or We're having problems with the family. And I'll say, Aw, I'll come in the morning. And they say, No, you come now." I asked him, "Where does your authority come from?" And he said, "From God. And the people. But I get up in the morning and I just let the Spirit move wherever, whatever I have to do. You couldn't plan your week, you couldn't plan your day, you just move how the Spirit moves you. And from the people. One minute you could be here, the next minute you're called somewhere else."

Here is authority as Received from God and the people. Howard Ashby's role is given to him. This traditional way of holding authority as primarily Received appears to be waning in our culture.

Received authority holds promise. We can't survive our early days or flourish in our later years without receiving. Receiving is essential to the religious life: Unless I become like a little child I cannot enter the kingdom. In the morning I spend some time sitting quietly with my hands open in my lap. I stand at the altar rail with my hands open to receive the sacrament. Going to church means letting someone else take over for an hour so I can know my dependence once again. "From God. And the people": Howard Ashby's obedience holds a profound beauty.

The authority that is "laid on" as part of the job promises us a place to start from and a shared understanding of what we are about. Susan Adams, another New Zealand Anglican priest, commented on the importance to her role of "people's expectation that you can reflect with them about the meaning of life and what's happening for them." Priest and people have a common assumption about what it is they are gathered to do. And Received authority reserves a place to fall back when the going gets too rough.

Received authority is the starting point for growing in authority, as Judith McMorland pointed out. As a continuing educator, she saw mature authority as

> the capacity to own your own authority, and to know from the inside who you are. And I think that's very much a developmental thing, like the capacity to be authoritative out of the base of one's own knowing. When you're teaching you have to get to a point of self-valuing in order to be able to express that... On the journey to getting to that place you also confront all the issues about who are

the authorities over you, and you have to have met them before you can get to the other place...

Received authority can also hold problems. When I am always subject to other people's authority or when I carry out a role just as it has been delivered to me, I may wake up to the discovery that I am behaving in a way that violates my own convictions. Susan Adams found herself impelled to question the authority she had received, to reinterpret it. "As a woman," she said passionately, "I'm trying to exercise authority in a different way." If my authority is totally shaped by the role I've been given, I will fail to develop my own selfhood and live out of my own center. I will avoid the risk and attendant anxiety of separation that is an inescapable part of "questioning the authorities." I may allow myself to remain passive and over-dependent on others' authority. John C. Harris described how passive clergy lived in fear of rocking the boat and displeasing parishioners. They had put their selves on the shelf.[3]

Women and men tend to experience different promises and problems with Received authority because women have been urged toward the receptive mode and men have been urged to deny that they received anything and bolt toward Autonomy. (We will examine men's and women's experiences with authority in more detail in Chapter 4.) Because the masculine way has often been assumed to be the human way, our culture tends to reject the Receiving posture in favor of the Autonomous stance. Our discomfort with simple receptivity impoverishes our spiritual life. Equating it with passivity, we regard all dependence with suspicion. In our distrust of dependence, we sometimes amputate our ties with others and model our authority on heroes like the Lone Ranger who, having suddenly appeared on the scene to strike a blow for justice, gallops off into the sunset before anyone can say "Thank you."

A question to think about: In your own experience of Received authority, what promise and what problems have you found?

2. Autonomous Authority

What makes us turn toward Autonomy? Usually the realization that we
can't depend on external authorities to take care of us gives birth to the
hopeful thought: "I can find my own authority within myself."[4]   We
can then begin to move from dependence on the authority of others to
confidence in our own internal authority.

When we discover that we are operating out of a role totally defined
by others, we encounter some of the difficulties experienced by Harris'
passive clergy. They began to realize that they were spending a lot of
time trying to look good. They always said yes. Preoccupied with ap-
peasing aggressive lay leaders, they hesitated to assert their own needs.
They backed away from challenging anybody, bracketed their own
convictions, and anxiously avoided getting clear about expectations and
accountability for their performance. As Harris worked with his clergy
group, a critical moment arrived: the pastors suddenly "saw the self-
destructive results of their behavior"—their eroded self-esteem, their
lowered energy, their helpless rage.[5] Reflecting on the group's work, one
pastor said, "The experience enabled me to see myself as a person distinct from the church for the first time since I left high school."[6]

When passivity is my problem, I need to embrace the promise of
discovering a more centered self. Inching into Autonomy, I begin to
discern some options beyond helplessness. I begin to define my own
reality instead of letting other people do it for me. I begin to see myself
as a person apart from others. And out of the shadows emerges a line
that marks where I stop and other people begin.

Like many clergy, Dee Crabtree had become acutely aware of the
importance of staying "clear about how much of what is being expressed
toward us is someone else's need. And not make it ours, not becoming
dependent on it." Distinguishing self from role affords freedom and
flexibility and a sense of inner sturdiness, as Joyce Yarrow discovered:
"When I was with the YWCA I realized that I felt that if I lost my job I
would have lost my life. Since that realization, I've done a lot of work
on coming to understand that my authority comes from me, not the position I hold, for my gifts are mine and they go with me no matter what
role I'm in."

Autonomous leaders not only claim freedom for themselves, they
may learn to offer it to others. Belenky et al. point out "that you must

first begin to hear your own inner voice in order to understand the importance of drawing out the voices of others..."[7] Interviewees spelled out how their own self-definition helped others be more fully themselves. "Who I am is not co-terminous with my role as a minister," said Dwight Lundgren. "And that allows them to be who they are also." The gifts of freedom to define oneself and accept one's own responsibilities are demanding gifts, as Lundgren observed:

> People will come to me out of a committee meeting and...it's clear to me what they're saying is "I don't want to have to say this to such-and-such a person; would you do it?" And I will not get in the middle of that kind of thing. I'll help them to see that that's a problem they're having. But they've accepted responsibility for this task and it's not going to kill them to exercise it.

Offering others Autonomy means forgoing the mutual satisfaction of answer-giving, emphasized Episcopal clergyman Jim Adams: "I have my answers. I know what works for me, but I can't hand my answers to other people, or I'll still be their authority."

Autonomous leaders' severe gifts benefit individuals and systems, too. Edwin Friedman points out that a leader who is fused with the system can have little or no effect on it.[8] Even our grammar spells out our Autonomy (or lack of Autonomy) as leaders. We have all struggled through the turgid prose of institutional communications couched in the passive voice: "It was felt that..."; "It has been decided..." Autonomous leaders don't hide behind passive prose; they make authority visible by taking responsibility for their decisions, announcing them legibly, and offering to explain and perhaps even to modify them.[9]

Autonomous authority exacts less subtle costs, as well. Keith Mason, whose support of women's ordination put him at odds with the Anglican Diocese of Sydney, found that bucking the system set him and his fellow advocates in a shaky place: "Being on the outskirts of the official authority and resenting what that official authority does breed a certain degree of insecurity within the group, and so you tend to cling to each other for mutual support." Strongly Autonomous leaders like Jim Adams may have to work hard to connect with other people:

> I err on the side of remoteness because of my personality. So whenever I am exposed as being a normal, awkward, blundering

human being people feel closer to me, and then they trust me more. They believe I will understand their foibles and weaknesses and failures because they can see mine. That's why in preaching I frequently try to find illustrations in which my ineptness can be held up to laughter.

Autonomous leaders can miss the mark. In our culture they often appear in the role of Expert (whom we often call an "Authority"). While we need and profit from the contributions of Experts, that role can be seductive. By definition, the Expert "knows," while the rest of us "don't know." Experts' knowledge gives them power, and we (and they) may want to believe they know more than they do. I remember the aura of arcane wisdom that swirled around the T-group trainer in group dynamics laboratories. Like a psychoanalyst, the trainer's perceived wisdom rose in proportion to his inscrutibility as we eagerly awaited the cryptic process observation that put a period on the training session. This power in separateness must have informed the old saw that "an expert is someone from out of town." We admire Experts because they seem self-sufficient. In the glorious isolation of his expertise, the Autonomous authority can get away with ignoring the rest of us and leaving the ordinary tasks of nurture to lesser souls.[10]

The lonely role of the Autonomous authority may deserve our respect and admiration; it's not easy to differentiate oneself from the herd and take tough stands. Yet the courage to take an unpopular position must be teased apart from a romantic love of loneliness for its own sake. Are we fascinated with the Lone Ranger because he strikes a blow for justice or because he doesn't need anybody else? In the loneliness of the priest's job, says Bruce Reed, "He experiences some of the aloneness of Christ on the cross." The priest drawn to such statements must also be drawn to discern whether the appeal lies in self-differentiation or self-dramatization.

Autonomy is the way to move out of unresolved dependence; but it's only one turn in the road—not the end of the journey. For mature authority is found not in isolation but in engagement.

Take a few minutes to reflect on the cost and promise of Autonomous authority in your own experience.

3. Assertive Authority

If my path seems to be trailing off toward isolation, I might try finding my way back to the human community and making a difference there. In a sense Assertion ushers in the active exercise of authority. When not heard, said Joyce Yarrow, "I take strength in my self and make that happen" (i.e., make it happen that she is heard). Assertion means moving outside oneself, reaching out with vigor and initiative, acting on the world.

Barry Evans, too, speaks of *taking* authority as he reaches toward the promise of Assertive authority. "The verb 'take' tries to get the flavor of 'taking a risk'"—it's "exciting and productive."[11] Tillich taps into the same vitality when he speaks of "the drive of everything living to realize itself with increasing intensity and extensity."[12] Joyce Yarrow has been able to realize herself more fully by taking opportunities "to risk a lot, to fail a lot, and to learn by that." Experiences "of getting knocked down and standing up again" have helped her develop self-confidence. Several interviewees' stories illustrated that primary strength of Assertive authority: the willingness to reach out with energy, take responsibility, and make things happen.

Responsibility is the primary promise of Assertive authority; Assertion becomes problematic when it edges over into *control*. (Now of course, all of us at some points have to claim control over our lives. Most of you have learned to do that. And there are situations in which the police have to take control. With that caveat in mind, I will henceforth use "controlling" to mean inappropriate domination of others.)

The positive move toward expressing myself actively in the world can easily shift into the darker mode of being myself all over the place. I get carried away with my agenda, and then "I'm not sensitive to where the other people are," as Judith McMorland confessed. I am failing to respect and honor the integrity and mystery of the other. And my pushing therefore, quite properly, arouses the other's resistance. When leaders say "I'm going to make a strong case for us changing," their pressure may carry the seed of its own defeat, observed Dorothy McMahon: "...If you set up a situation where people have to defend themselves against the dream, then you're behind the eightball to start with..."

In my role as advocate, I often discover that my separate, active posture has become an "I win and you lose" posture. Pushing other people around takes a predictable toll on my relationships with them. Ken Kesey paints a horrifying picture of control in the character of Big Nurse in *One Flew Over the Cuckoo's Nest*: she takes responsibility, all right, but she does so in a way that diminishes other people and destroys their freedom. Do you remember her? A "full-breasted tyrant" in a "crackling white uniform," she strides down the hall crashing patients out of her way with a swing of her big wicker bag. If anyone gets in her way, she is tied into "a white knot of tight-smiled fury."[13]

Those Experts we considered earlier may be not only Autonomous but controlling in their separate power. Experts have the capacity not only to help but to disempower. As Belenky and her colleagues pointed out, Experts can "assert dominance over less knowledgeable people either by assaulting them with information or by withholding information."[14] In the church, for example, the expertise of "professional" clergy defines the laity as "unprofessional."

When authority really means *control* in church settings, a number of difficulties are set in motion. Leaders become more interested in being right than being helpful. Religious leaders who grab all the authority find themselves crushed by the burden of such a load of responsibility. They then end up overloaded, resentful, and treading the burnout road. The lay people, on the other hand, find themselves disrespected and disempowered. We become dulled to the way this state of affairs contradicts the church's stated values, as Kierkegaard saw:

> the honorable Right Reverend General Superintendent Minister stands up in the cathedral and announces as his text: "God hath elected the base things of the world and the things that are despised," and yet nobody laughs. (*Attack Upon Christendom*)

The culture beyond the church is also dominated by Control. The Control culture promotes loyalty toward the in-group and hostility toward the out-group. It becomes natural to divide people into winners and losers. Why would you consider welcoming the marginal ones, when you have proved you're superior to them and have rooted out the weaknesses that hold them back? According to a recent survey, white men believe that if others (women and minorities) win better positions, the men will lose out.[15] If all power is arranged in pyramids, they are right.

The Control culture provides a comfortable haven for the Authoritarian Personality. In a world structured by control and ranking, the Authoritarian Personality feels secure. Within the hierarchy of power, he has his own niche. While he must submit to those above him, he can tell those below him what to do.

People at the Assertive stage and people at the Receiving stage can lock together in a symbiotic arrangement that relieves both of the challenge of living in the tension between those two postures. The Receptive one doesn't have to assert herself and the Assertive one doesn't have to admit he needs to receive anything.

In your own experience of Assertive authority, what works well? What do you want to question?

Here's an exercise that will help you lay the groundwork for the next section. Get drawing materials. Think of a graceful moment in exercising your authority—a time when it all flowed. Get in touch with that experience. Savor it for a moment.

Is there a metaphor or symbol that comes to you about that experience? It was like...What? Take colors and paper and make a picture of that moment or that symbol. (If drawing reminds you of a trauma in your second grade art class, substitute a poem, dance, mime, etc.)

If you are carrying out this reflection process in a colleague or support group, a "show and tell" session, sharing pictures and graceful moments, can be an affirming, revealing, team-building exercise.

Received authority, Autonomous authority, Assertive authority: the strengths of these three stages find their fruition in the movement they trace toward wholeness. The problem lies in getting stuck in any of them and losing sight of the value of the others. Assertive people may look back and conclude that they have arrived. They congratulate themselves on having pulled themselves out of dependence. The pattern of growth looks like a simple developmental hierarchy from the top of the Assertive mountain—every day, in every way, better and better! Yet they can't see ahead to the other side of that mountain. But wait! When people construe life as a hierarchical progression, with themselves at the apex, we can conclude that "one thing more is needed." If you can't give it up, you're stuck at the level of Control.

One woman said: "I don't know what it means to live without

controlling other people and being controlled, but I want to find out."
Dorothy McMahon reflects on an experience that helped her find out:

> At one time when I was quite seduced by the hierarchical power of
> the church, I served on a national evangelism committee with [a
> colleague]. Up until this point, my friend and I hadn't entered into
> the wheeling and dealing, but now we reflected with each other on
> whether we would try to get our nomination onto a particular com-
> mittee in order to shift its direction. We worked out a clever way of
> lobbying for our nominee that wasn't exactly tricky, but it was a
> power play. It was really quite hilarious: as soon as the meeting
> started, we started maneuvering to get our person onto the commit-
> tee, while the others also jockeyed for power—and we won! At that
> minute, we knew we now had an entirely different relationship with
> the other members of the committee. And the difference was this:
> they were no longer afraid of our power because we were playing
> the same game as they were, whereas before we had always been
> just authentically ourselves, pushing for our objectives in a totally
> direct way without playing any games. When we came away
> laughing from the meeting, my friend said to me, "Those who live
> by the sword shall die by the sword." And we both knew what that
> meant. We realized that real...authority was linked with straightfor-
> ward integrity, and that we had been recognized as much stronger
> on that team before we took up bureaucratic methods of power and
> authority... And we realized that we had laid that down for another
> sort of power and authority.

4. Integrated Authority

From Assertion to Integration: A Difficult Boundary

Guided by psychologists, many of us devote a good deal of attention and
effort to making the transition from Received authority to Autonomous
authority. It takes a lot of insight, courage, and energy to move from a
posture in which other people call the shots to a willingness to exercise
control over my own life from within. The movement from Assertion to
Integration appears to be a shift in the opposite direction. No wonder we

resist what feels like an invitation to abandon our hard-won internal control. It feels all *wrong*. It sounds like slipping backward.

Many gospel stories show Jesus trying to help people move from an Assertive to an Integrated posture. They don't understand. They resist. They get angry. They go away bewildered and sad. People in a Control culture, feeling that they have finally gotten on top of the situation, find it hard to imagine they might give that up and move on to a new way of living that promises greater rewards. But some do "get it." The new perspective breaks through with a shock, and flips the old assumptions on their heads.

Mark paints a dramatic picture of this collision of expectations in the story of the anointing at Bethany, sandwiched between accounts of a plot by the authorities and the betrayal of an insider. Jesus has been unable to correct his disciples' assumption that he is the messiah who is to come in power.

> While he was at Bethany in the house of Simon the leper, as he sat at the table, a woman came with an alabaster jar of very costly ointment of nard, and she broke open the jar and poured the ointment on his head. But some were there who said to one another in anger, "Why was the ointment wasted in this way? For this ointment could have been sold for more than three hundred denarii, and the money given to the poor." And they scolded her. But Jesus said, "Let her alone; why do you trouble her? She has performed a good service for me. For you always have the poor with you, and you can show kindness to them whenever you wish; but you will not always have me. She has done what she could; she has anointed my body beforehand for its burial. Truly I tell you, wherever the good news is proclaimed in the whole world, what she has done will be told in remembrance of her." (Mk. 14:3-9)

Jesus' dramatic repudiation of the dinner guests' assumptions is signaled by the anger and conflict in the story. We come upon scenes like this again and again: Jesus pairing with one who has no power— frequently, as in this case, a woman of the common people—in contradicting the expectations of the Control culture. The woman is simply receiving Jesus' message about himself, and dramatically symbolizing it in a prophetic act. The royal anointing of Jesus' head is at the same time an anointing for burial. Kelber describes the paradoxical truth revealed in this act: "He is anointed not by the priests or the high priest but by an anonymous woman. His anointment is not applauded but criticized. Above all, he is not anointed to power and life but 'beforehand for the burial' (14:8)...his purpose is not to fulfil traditional Davidic expectations but to upset and reverse them."[16] Those whose frame of reference stops with control cannot accept the paradoxical truth her action prophesies: the king is the crucified one.

The story seems to tell us that following Jesus means embracing a different kind of authority: standing in opposition to "what everybody knows," and breaking through to a new, paradoxical way of seeing. What are some of these new understandings that lie beyond Control?

Authority Belongs to God.

The Bible says clearly that all authority belongs to God. In our day, however, we don't hear as much about the authority of God as we do about the power of God. When we talk about the power of God, we are often expressing our concern that God's power is a *problem* for us: God is acting in ways that seem not to be in our interest, and we are attempting to reconcile the discrepancy. At other times we speak about the power of God as released through us in the form of *energy*. But our thinking about authority suffers because we seldom focus on the *authority* of God, and because we lack a clear concept of authority as distinct from power. What would it mean for us to focus on *authority as belonging to God*?

The clearest message I have received from studying the gospels' (particularly the Fourth Gospel's) picture of authority is that *authority is given by God:* given by the Father to the Son, given by Jesus to the disciples, and handed on by them to other followers of Jesus. And the interviewees make it clear that holding their authority as given by God means holding it *differently*.

This differentness had different flavors for different people. For Verna Dozier, authority is held *in trust*. "Does what you have been telling me about you and your authority remind you of any Bible stories?" I asked. She answered: "And God called Abraham. God said, 'I will bless you in order that you may be a blessing.' Authority is a gift to

be used. For God, for God's people. And I think it is a blessing." For
Peter Sherer, the givenness of his authority means *not being alone.*
When troubled by doubts about his competence, said Peter, "I put myself
in churchy circumstances." What happens there? "I'm reminded that I
might not be running the railroad by myself." For Dwight Lundgren,
God-given authority can be held only with *an awe-filled lightness.*
Describing what a minister does to act on his authority, Dwight added:
"...and to do it with kind of a lightness. I really like Woody Allen's
movies. He's always thinking about all these profound things, and doing
it by keeping things light. We're talking about *God*! What do *we* know
about God? *We're* the ones who are saying [these things], and so we'd
better be fairly light about it."

If authority belongs to God, a shift to Integrated authority means a
shift from willfulness to willingness. Look at the authority of the "authorities" in the Gospel stories and then at the authority of Jesus. "I have
come down from heaven, not to do my own will but the will of him who
sent me." (Jn. 7:38) And in Gethsemane: "Abba, Father, for you all
things are possible; remove this cup from me; yet, not what I want, but
what you want." (Mk. 14:36) An assertive request. Yet a total surrender
of willfulness. In this passage Schweizer points out: "'I' and 'you,' Son
and Father, are set in contrast to each other but are united in the submis-
sion of obedience."[17]

God's ownership and "manifold delegation" of authority give
people the message that authority is not a scarce but an abundant commodity. If they are "clothed with power from on high" (Lk. 24:49) the
disciples don't have to ration it. Authority as given by God through
Jesus and then passed on flows out from within, out of one's own essence, out in self-emptying. What a different picture from the kind of
authority we carve chunks of and hang on to! This abundant authority is
not the same as getting our own way. We *can't all* get our own way; but
we can all live with authority. And if God doesn't control people, and it
is God's authority that we are exercising, our own authority has been
given a special kind of shaping.

Integrated authority doesn't depend on Control.

If authority belongs to God, perhaps we can loosen our grip on control.

Authority begins to look like cooperating with Life (and other people) instead of trying to be on top of it. We entertain the possibility that after all we aren't called to be "on top of" life, but to be in it, faithfully.

Jim Adams reflects:

> I have no control... But I have more and more authority... Authority doesn't mean getting your way... Sometimes [parishioners] agree and sometimes they disagree. And sometimes they do what I want and sometimes they don't. But even when they disagree or don't do what I want, they haven't diminished my authority as a religious leader... I don't feel I've got the kind of authority that an army general or the CEO of a corporation has. I wouldn't know what to do with it if I did.

Dorothy McMahon talks about authority as being "taken right down into one's humanness. I've discovered with joy and amazement that sometimes I have the greatest authority when my own life is at its most vulnerable. When I've been prepared to say I have failed and I am about to fail... I have discovered that that is the moment when people recognize my ministry."

One way we often try to achieve control is by being *right*. Verna Dozier has arrived at a conviction that salvation does not lie in being right: "As a young person I was very authoritative, and when I said something it was *right*, and I would brook no opposition. And there's still some of that there, you know." In her seventies, however, Verna has come to realize

> that people are not convinced by words, and there are some people for whom I am going to be the messenger, and for other people I'm not going to be the messenger, and I can't be the messenger for everybody. And I am not destroyed when someone says, "You're wrong." I've had people walk out on a Bible session, and sometimes it's a lot of fun... I try not to pull my rank as the visiting Bible expert, or the great guru of the Bible... I am more and more convinced that if what we really want is for everybody to know they are worthy and valued, we have to have a relationship with them at all times that affirms that.

And so very often, even when she thinks someone is absolutely wrong, Verna says, "I just let it go."

Many people report an "aha" when they discover that authority is not about control—that control may even get in the way of true authority. Members of AA describe surrendering control as a transforming event. I have discovered that as I give up control over my grown children I have more authority. When I stop trying to tell them how to live their lives, sometimes they even ask me what I think! Working with a clergy group, I remember an unusual experience: as I spoke about "inhabiting our longings" my voice broke and my eyes filled with tears. In the post-meeting comments, several people spoke about the "grace-filled moment" when the insight came that "living with the longing—not getting what I want and living in the emptiness—leaves room for God." In our work with congregations in The Alban Institute, we frequently find that out-of-control moments are moments when a life-giving possibility might break through: new insight, a new direction, new power to move out of a stuck place.

But it is not easy to break through the barriers we erect against the surrender of control. Jesus tried every way he could think of to get his disciples to understand that he was not the powerful messiah they expected, but the suffering Son of Man. Because they couldn't imagine giving up control, many people could not comprehend the challenges with which he presented them. And so they turned sorrowfully and went away.

Surrendering control goes against our grain. Sometimes it seems possible only at those places where we *give up* authority. After his resignation, Shevardnadze reflected, "Now for the first time I realize how much authority I have in my own country." We see such authority without control as a contradiction in terms, which betrays our unthinking identification of authority with control. The testimony of people like Jim Adams and Dorothy McMahon and Verna Dozier and Eduard Shevardnadze suggests how we can distinguish authority from control.

Hierarchy is not the point.

James and John, the sons of Zebedee, came forward to him and said to him, "Teacher, we want you to do for us whatever we ask of

you...Grant us to sit, one at your right hand and one at your left, in
your glory." But Jesus said to them, "You do not know what you
are asking."...[The other disciples] began to be angry with James
and John. So Jesus called them and said to them, "You know that
among the Gentiles those whom they recognize as their rulers lord it
over them. And their great ones are tyrants over them. But it shall
not be so among you; but whoever wishes to become great among
you must be your servant, and whoever wishes to be first among
you must be slave of all. For the Son of Man came not to be served
but to serve, and to give his life a ransom for many." (Mk. 10:35,
37—38a, 41-45)

Here is another story of conflict. James and John are angling for a higher
position on the ladder of the new administration: they want to be the
vice-presidents. The other disciples quite naturally respond by trying to
shove the pushy ones off that rung. Wrong! All of you! comes the reply
from Jesus. Your authority is to be of a new kind. Jesus' way turns all
human patterns of authority on their heads. "Who's going to win?" is not
the question; we're invited to play an entirely new game.

The whole hierarchical structure is off target. "It shall not be so
among you." In this new game, those who want to be great are not those
who can scramble up the ladder first, but those who do what's needed—
for everybody.

Integrated authority honors the freedom of the other.

Martin Luther said, "A Christian man is the most free lord of all, and
subject to none; a Christian man is the most dutiful servant of all, and
subject to everyone." People who exercise Integrated authority claim for
everyone the freedom that the Autonomous leader claims for himself.
Because they include and invite my autonomy, I don't have to stand on
guard protecting it. In contrast with all the other "authorities" we read
about in the gospel stories, Jesus' authority liberates people.

Interviewees told stories about graceful moments (like the moment
you may have recalled in response to the suggestion on page 23) when
their authority embraced and enhanced other people's freedom. Susan
Adams said: "Grace is that people give you the authority willingly that

you have been assigned by role." She perceived that (in Weber's words) "we can always tell when a sense of authority exists in a society; it is when people *voluntarily* obey their rulers."[18]

Peter Sherer described a recent graceful period in his work with the National Community AIDS Partnership: "The last eighteen months I have been trying to persuade a key group of people that my version of the future is the appropriate one. They are not only agreeing with it but willing to play their part in making it happen... I feel...a profound sense of joy that now I can play a much less stress-producing role: I can cheerlead but I don't have to be so fierce; I can be playful and let them know what a great idea they had; instead of being scout leader, it's a game of volleyball and they all came to play, and I brought the ball and I don't have to be the captain."

The following bit of conversation gives us a glimpse of how a follower experienced this authority that makes way for the autonomy of others. Jim Adams was reflecting on how his ministry was evolving: "I have no control... But I have more and more authority." A parishioner responded: "That authority frees me up to be myself and make decisions."[19]

With Integrated authority, stages become styles.

Any developmental hierarchies people may have thought they were climbing now seem aside from the point. Moving from Assertive to Integrated authority means leaving "stages" behind. Growth now seems more like the gathering of one richness upon another; there is less sense of "this is something to achieve and then get beyond." Ladder metaphors imply that we are stepping off one rung onto a higher one. In contrast, Integrated authority is more likely to say "yes" to everything that went before. This reaching out for maturity by building on beginnings is like a sapling, which adds yearly rings on its way to becoming a fully grown tree. Perhaps "rings" provide a more helpful metaphor than "rungs." While people do often seem to grow by moving from Received, through Autonomous and Assertive authority, to Integrated authority, people whose authority is Integrated affirm all those ways of being authoritative, both within themselves and in other people. It all depends on what's needed. As Joyce Yarrow looked back on the development of her authority, she saw that she now had several options: she can now choose to work "in a collaborative mode, in an assertive mode, or whatever may be needed."

People with Integrated authority can respond in any of those ways, depending on the requirements of the situation, but they may prefer to function in primarily Receptive, Autonomous, or Assertive modes.

These people *experience* their authority as Integrated.

Those who exercise Integrated authority experience their authority as Received, Autonomous, Assertive, and Integrated—all at the same time. The contradictions fade away. It's like "all the rivers running to the sea," reflected Verna Dozier. For Dee Crabtree, "The integration is internal. It's the coming together of all those skills and perspectives that I have in me."

Dee sees that integration not only within her but between her and her parishioners: "I believe the Holy Spirit is calling every ordained minister beyond timidity and beyond control into a new life lived in rich relationship with those who are called the laity."[20] Susan Adams found an image for that contextual quality of authority-grounded-in-community in "a flowering shrub." For her a growing pot plant of the sort some- times given to her by her women's group "says something about the sort of rootedness within the group and within the historical development of the church and the women's movement within it and its ability to pro- duce blooms and flowers and last for a very long time."

What is going on inside these leaders is integrated with the situation around them. Judith McMorland, continuing educator and Anglican laywoman, incarnated this aspect of Integrated authority in her account of a commonplace task: "when we were looking at the diocese in re- view... I'd been asked by the bishop to be on that committee because I'd been very rude about the clergy anyhow, and had made a lot of noises... But...we...claimed within the group to do it differently...it all just flowed wonderfully... Everybody was fully there on their own authority. There wasn't any sense of not being peers, but we had different skills..."

Integrated authority is often marked by humor and lightness ("I'd been very rude about the clergy"), signs of an inner easiness which stands in contrast to anxious reactivity.

Integrated authority is tensive and paradoxical.

Either/or has become both/and; what had appeared to be opposites no longer stand in painful contradiction. People whose authority is Integrated now seem able to live in the tension between inner and outer realities and between receptive and active postures. We could diagram the progression, as people move deeper between the poles of both those tensions, in this way:

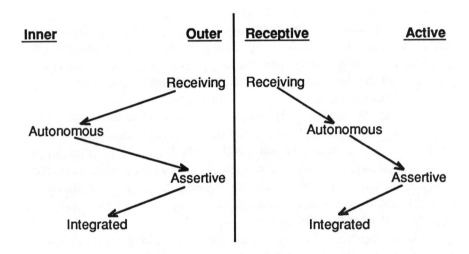

People with Integrated authority seem to have a different vision of *truth* and a lightened sense of *control*. Verna Dozier, who remembers her earlier concern to be *right*, now reflects, "I realize that...there are some people for whom I am going to be the messenger, and for other people I'm not going to be the messenger... And I am not destroyed when someone says, 'You're wrong.'" Many interviews revealed this shift from the *rightness* of Assertive authority to the Integrated quality of *lightness* and tolerance for ambiguity. When people are willing to let go of control, they are no longer so upset by paradoxical statements; they can even appreciate the mystery which paradox enshrines. They have broken out of the Control culture's compulsion to stack truth up in neat pyramids that leave no room for unknowing.

We could describe the paradoxical and tensive quality of Integrated authority in many ways. I want to develop one in some detail: *Integrated*

authority means living in the tension between exousia (literally living
"out of one's own essence or being") and kenosis (self-emptying).

The literal meaning of *exousia*—"out of being" or "out of one's own
being"—the Greek word for authority used in the New Testament, might
suggest in today's terms that people with authority are operating out of a
centered self. The apostolic call to each person is "to be the most
uniquely oneself."[21]

"For he taught them as one who had authority and not as the scribes"
(Mt. 7:29).

"But *I* say to you..." (Mt. 5:29)

The picture of Jesus' authority stands in contrast to that of the
scribes, who pointed elsewhere, grounding their authority in the external
"authorities" to whom they appealed in order to justify their positions.
Jesus claims that his authority is "from heaven" not "from people."
Walter Wink suggests that thinking of the sources of authority as "inside" or "outside" may be more useful for us today than the up/down
metaphor of "heaven" or "earth."[22] (Is the kingdom of heaven "within"
you?) "Inside" touches the infinite without the hierarchical implications
in "up" or "down." People whose authority comes from within can carry
their authority into any role or situation, as Judith McMorland discovered: "I find myself within situations where I'm seen to be authoritative
regardless of what the context is."

We can find the other pole of the paradox in Philippians 2:6-7,
where Paul says Christ Jesus, "though he was in the form of God...
emptied himself, taking the form of a slave." Self-emptying means a
willingness to be transparent for the Holy One who "has renounced rule
for servanthood and calls us to do the same."[23] When we stop being full
of ourselves, we can make space for the other in our hearts and in daily
human interchange. In the picture of Jesus (for example, in John's gospel or even Matthew's) we can see echoes of divine Wisdom, or Sophia,
the hostess who offers hospitable space to all. Jesus' going away su-
premely expresses his willingness to make room for the authority of his
friends.

Interviewees describe "self-emptying" in very down-to-earth terms.
When they have a role of authority in a group, they put limits on their
own self-expression in order to evoke the authority of other members.
In their role, leaders set aside for a time their own need to Receive; they
give up some of their Autonomy and Assertiveness for the sake of the

people they are called to serve. They hold their authority tensively—as having yet not having—never with an iron fist. Keith Mason was acutely aware of the danger "that the ultimate issue becomes your authority rather than the task at hand or the long-term happiness of the unit or the child." Keeping first things first meant holding his authority lightly. Dee Crabtree described the kenotic role of a pastor as counselor: "I become a mirror and they become able to see themselves with greater clarity because I have stayed clear, and times like that are the juiciest, most fruitful pastoral ministry that I have known... If I am willing to stand there and let them hit up against me for a while...people are able to make many more breakthroughs in their own lives." Dorothy McMahon intentionally undercuts parishioners' assumptions about her exalted role in the congregation and their dependence on her: "I keep undermining that perception of who I am. I scrub the floor with them when we scrub the floor. I wash the dishes. I do flowers with the women, and so on, so that I cut across roles all the time."

The picture of Jesus in the gospels brings these two themes together in a dynamic paradox: exousia *and* kenosis, self-definition *and* self-emptying. At Caesarea Philippi his clear self-definition is outlined by the sharp edges of rebuke between himself and Peter. Then he says, "those who want to save their life will lose it." (Mk. 8:27-9:1) Similarly in John's gospel the footwashing story dramatizes the paradox of exousia and kenosis:

> And during supper Jesus, knowing that the Father had given all things into his hands, and that he had come from God and was going to God, got up from the table, took off his outer robe, and tied a towel around himself. Then he poured water into a basin and began to wash the disciples' feet...(Jn. 13:3-4)

The two parts of the sentence, "knowing that the Father had given all things into his hands" and "tied a towel around himself," are connected and paradoxical statements that, when joined in one sentence, vividly convey the gospels' picture of authority. Doing the work of a slave is not an action of passivity and powerlessness in this story, because it is the action of one who "knows" and whose hands hold "all things." This doing-for-another is a *chosen* act—not of an unfree person but of a most free person. In the Control culture, those who "have" and "know" act like masters, not servants. But in his joining of exousia and kenosis, Jesus is seen to be most authoritative when he is "most transparent to the sources of his selfhood."[24] The uniqueness of his authority is seen in his eagerness to give it away to his friends.

The tension between self-definition and self-emptying takes practical shape as Jim Adams describes his work in the light of this gospel picture:

> In the unfolding story we can see the way the disciples discovered their own authority in spite of themselves because Jesus refused to be the answer for them. That's the power of the story of Jesus, "who thought equality with God not a thing to be grasped but emptied himself," and became one of us.

I asked, "What would emptying yourself look like? Adams replied:

> It's being willing in [an adult] confirmation class to have people get annoyed and upset with me because I won't take care of them in the way they think I should. It feels very empty. I sit there helplessly knowing there really is nothing I can do that would be genuinely helpful, except to get out of their way. And it's being willing to sit with a person whose life is a mess and know I can't straighten him out. I go over to see Suzanne Cooper. She doesn't want to die. She keeps reviving. There isn't anything I can do for Suzanne Cooper. I just go over there and feel helpless—not just "feel," but *be* helpless, acknowledge the helplessness that's there. Those are the times when I think that to some extent I really am allowing God's authority to hold me up, rather than my own. I feel most authentically held together by God in the moments when I am willing to acknowledge my emptiness.

To give out of my own being and to empty myself to make space for the other—I experience those paradoxical calls in the humdrum tasks of leadership; every time I plan and lead a session, for instance. Usually I find myself, at best, responding to one call at the expense of the other. But sometimes, when I speak my own truth, but not from above, there emerges a graced and open space in which others can claim and articulate their own truth.

Paradox and tension mark, not only the experience of individuals as they discover Integrated authority, but the *process* of congregational life, as John C. Harris points out: "Creative tension is essential to the life-giving process of parish life."[25] When communities are willing to explore the territory beyond control, they discover more options, have to make more choices, and therefore feel more anxious. Churches willing to live in tension will find themselves more open to the ambiguities of authority and less subject to the reactive "rubberbanding" by which religious communities artificially simplify their options. Instead of flopping from one generation's fad which says "leaders are enablers" to the next generation's backlash—"I'm going to *take charge* here!"—church leaders may choose a more complex, situationally focused openness. As they ask, "What's needed here?" they can hear and respond to the contradictory calls.

Integrated authority brings together Received, Autonomous, and Assertive strengths.

The serenity to Receive, the courage to be Assertive, and the Autonomy to discern are all present options.

People with Integrated authority can be receptive again. Those who are consistently Assertive hold dependence and vulnerability at bay and dissect the muddle of winning and losing that marks human experience into "I win and you lose." Integrated authority now transcends that reactive posture and welcomes back the receptive, the marginal—within the self and within others, too. The marginal within me and the "little one" out there are connected, as Jung saw: "But what if I should discover that the least amongst them all... are within me?"[26]

We can see this welcome dramatized in stories of Jesus' encounters with marginal people—particularly children. To the disciples, arguing about who was the greatest, Jesus responds by taking a little child in his arms and saying, "Whoever receives one such child in my name receives me; and whoever receives me, receives not me but him who sent me." (Mk. 9:33-37 RSV) Jesus' model of receptiveness is emphasized by the repetition of the verb "to receive" four times in the passage. "Little ones," marginal ones, are not to be despised; on the contrary they represent lifegiving possibilities for those captured by Control. Do you want to be born again? Then go back and touch your dependence again, and become like a child.

I see that same receptive quality, which is basic to the religious life, in the story that ends Mark's gospel: the women, overcome by emotion, flee the empty tomb, saying nothing to anyone. Perhaps those who say the story couldn't have stopped there because the women don't *do* anything are overlooking the simple appropriateness of "amazement and holy awe"[27] to this astonishing happening. The women's response reminds me of Job's answer to the God of the whirlwind: "What shall I answer thee? I lay my hand on my mouth." (Job 40:4) When faced with such an astounding theophany, what can we do but try to take it in? Such "holy awe" forms the appropriate foundation for the infant church's subsequent life and activity.

The willingness to be dependent and ask for help is an essential element in Integrated authority. Religious leaders follow a Lord who said "I can do nothing on my own." (John 5:30) They are on friendly terms with the weakness in which their power is made perfect. Interviewees ground their authority in their dependence on God. Dorothy McMahon discovered her greatest authority "when my own life is at its most vulnerable." Jim Adams points to moments of grace as "the times when I think that to some extent I really am allowing God's authority to hold me up, rather than my own."

Autonomy is recaptured—now dedicated to Integrated purposes. When phones begin to ring and lines form at the study door, young pastors can find it a heady experience! John Fletcher described how clergy finally wake up from the enchantment that set in when they found themselves regarded as powerful helpers. The pastor who emerges from that "madness of God" becomes centered once again in dependence upon God and in his own authenticity.[28] Those who have become fascinated with the exercise of their own power and have become alienated from their inner world now ground themselves once again in the internal dimensions of Receiving and Autonomy. Their uncritical expectation that they will do great things ceases to dominate their lives.

"They have no wine" evokes the self-differentiated response "Woman, what concern is that to you and to me? My hour has not yet come." (See Jn. 2:1-11) This reply of "simple disengagement," literally "What to me and to you?" is sometimes used "when someone is asked to get involved in a matter which he feels is no business of his" says

Raymond Brown.[29] Jesus is not going to do miracles because his mother tells him to. Neither natural family ties nor the opportunity to do something spectacular can provoke an automatic response. This picture reveals no compulsion either to engage or to disengage.

Autonomy is an essential ingredient in the Integrated way of living with authority, but it is no longer the be all and end all it may have seemed earlier. The Integrated leader acts with awareness that her autonomy holds benefits for others, extending to them also freedom and space to grow. "Do not hold on to me," says Jesus to Mary Magdalene at the moment of recognition outside the empty tomb. "But go to my brothers and say to them, 'I am ascending to my Father and your Father, to my God and your God.'" (Jn. 20:17-18) With her response to Jesus' "Go" Mary becomes the apostle. Her extradependence becomes intradependence. John often gathers up many people's experience in the drama of one person's story. With his command "Don't hang on to me—Go!" the risen Lord presses all his disciples toward a new relationship. As the sisters and brothers of the firstborn, "they will be sent as the Son is sent...and they will have the power...that he had," says Brown.[30] The Receptive moment of recognition has now evolved into a new Autonomy.

Integrated leaders speak "the word of God with boldness" (Acts 4:31). They don't slip back into passivity, under the hopeful misnomer of "enablement." "Boldness" demonstrates inner integration and contrasts with the "driving with the brakes on" that betrays a conflicted heart. The purpose of Assertiveness, however, is serving, not winning.

Dorothy McMahon has come to see that simple rejection of power is not a faithful response.

> I believe the church and its ministry must face up to the responsibility of actually exercising authority. I understand that very much as authentically struggling to name the Word, to name what is the Gospel for us at this moment—and a recognition that one will not always be right about that, for we see dimly. But to pull away from that is in fact to betray your calling, and it often flows over into your pastoral work too where you hesitate to say, with great authority, that God is at the bottom of every abyss.

Integrated leaders don't abdicate their Assertiveness in order to empower others, but instead encourage their followers toward Assertion, too.

Religious leaders can invite others to join them in becoming co-authors of the faith. Received faith is only the beginning. To what we have been given we join our struggles, the power of our experiences, our fresh articulation of what matters. The boldness with which we accept the challenge to become "authors" lights a fire, not only for us, but for our whole religious community. So for those with Integrated Authority, Assertiveness, authorship, energy, and boldness—far from being abdicated—kindle new energy in the whole living body.

People with Integrated authority evoke and enhance the authority of others.

There's plenty of authority to go around. It's not a fixed quantity so that if you get more, I'll have less. If leaders share it, authority increases and sources of energy expand. Ruth Shinn delights in the expectant quality of this open-handed authority: "You never know what member of the group is going to do something that is just right. And I like that. And that's why I enjoy a moderating role more than a directing role." Thus, in dramatic contrast to the Expert whose authority is predicated on others' lack of it, leaders with Integrated authority are always arranging spaces in which other people's authority can be born. Dwight Lundgren finds a pattern for his ministry in Barnabas, the "encourager and hospitality person":

> I said at the beginning of my ministry that one of the things I wanted to do in preaching was not just come with reports about what scripture is all about, but help people feel comfortable with handling it themselves, so that they feel as I'm working in it, "Oh *that's* how you do that"...

People with Integrated authority can inhabit a wider world.

Someone else is healing, Lord—should we stop him? Here is a small encounter between the "in-group" outlook of the culture of Control and the universal outlook of Integrated authority. The in-group provides padding for the ego; it's a buffer against whatever is being rejected within and projected without. All prior stages have carved up reality, embracing part of it and pushing away the rest (this also means that they accept some people and reject the rest). Integrated authority can be universal precisely because it's not reactive to the parts of human life (and the people) represented by earlier stages. When we have grown up to Integrated authority we can inhabit a wider world because we can tolerate contradictions and let go our anxious need to draw the circle so small that we can control it.

We might think of the movement toward Integrated authority as an outward spiral:

Receiving: I am part of the whole, receiving.

Autonomous: I am distinct.

Assertive: I am an actor in the world.

Integrated: I am part of the whole, giving.

If Love pervades the universe, I can live in it as ultimately a trustworthy, not a hostile place.

Conclusion

How can you and I tend to our own maturing in authority? It's a paradoxical road, and the answers that seemed useful at one turn may not help us at the next. We need to attend faithfully to the stretch of road we are travelling now. Any conceptual scheme like that provided in this chapter, of course, gives us only an artificially simplified guide to the intricate complexities of the journey. We go backward and forward; every event has many dimensions; we find ourselves at different stages in different aspects of our lives, as well as in stable or stressful conditions. No struggle of any stage is entirely foreign to my experience now.

You may, however, find some helpful clues in these patterns of growth. If you conclude that your authority is primarily Received, you may want to attend to the call to clarify your sense of your own uniqueness, your own point of view. There may be ways you now want to define yourself as different from what "everybody" expects.

If you find yourself primarily at the bend in the road called "Autonomous," you may want to evaluate the advantages and disadvantages of your separate stance and listen for a call to move out and start making a difference in some part of the world.

If Assertiveness seems the primary mark of your authority, you may be experiencing some tension from clenching the fist of control. Pay attention to your discomfort. Listen to your body more carefully. Notice whether you feel driven. Take a clear-eyed look at the people who arouse your contempt. Take some time to hear the inner voices that may have grown faint. It may be time to open that clenched hand.

If you often find that you can exercise your authority flexibly as the situation requires, relax and give yourself to the ministry where you are, making the choices that are now open to you, and enjoying your preferred style of exercising authority.

This prayer by Janet Morley speaks to me of that longed-for wholeness; perhaps it will speak to you.

> God our mother,
> You hold our life within you;
> nourish us at your breast,
> and teach us to walk alone.
> Help us to receive your tenderness
> and respond to your challenge
> that others may draw life from us,
> in your name, Amen.[31]

Journal exercise:

> *Where am I?*
> *What do I celebrate?*
> *What's missing?*
> *What might the next step look like for me?*
> *Where are the openings?*

CHAPTER III

Practical Dilemmas in the Exercise of Authority

Now that we have outlined patterns of growth in authority in a general way, let's shift gears and examine specific circumstances in which we must decide how to behave. Conceptual schemes make life look clearer than it is; in this chapter we will return to the murky multiplicity of daily experience as it presents itself to us in all its Monday-morning complications and concreteness. Each of us can gain practical understanding of how to exercise Integrated authority by looking closely at actual pressure points like these:

—when I have to decide whether to focus on getting the job done or caring for the people, or (even harder) whether to risk compromising my vision or jeopardizing my solidarity with my people

—when others challenge my authority head on

—when my sense of myself and my role seem to be at odds

—or when I have to wrestle with the discrepancy between my own view of my authority and the projections that come filtered through others' longings and fears.

When "the moment to decide" is upon me, my authority is put to the test, and I am forced to discern what matters most—and then to act.

My Leadership Style: Do I Emphasize the People or the Task?

As leaders, we want to get the job done. And we want to behave in a way that is respectful and caring toward the people with whom we work. I asked the interviewees, "Do you tend to focus on the task more or to support the people you're working with more?" Some replied "the task," others "the people"; and still others told how they found the contradiction between task and people overcome. Let's imagine that we are eavesdropping while several of these interviewees sit around a table exploring all the dimensions of the tension between task and people that emerge in their daily experience.

A couple of them open the conversation by saying they focus on "the people." Colin Bradford, the international economist, explains why he emphasizes what is happening for the people, their energy, and their commitment, even more than getting the task done:

> How you get a group somewhere is as important as where you get them to. And how self-determining they are in the process is to me a very important part of it. In other words I don't like a situation in which there's a kind of forced march to a predetermined destination... I tend to like more sensitive leadership that responds also to where the group wants to go and energizes the group as a result, so the group ends up being more than it might otherwise be because you evoke commitment on the part of the group towards where you're going... I'm looking for high energy.

Jim Adams also pays more attention to the people, admitting that the people's energetic "being the church" has proved more important than getting his own way.

Life-long teacher Verna Dozier calls our attention to the other side of the tension: "I really focus on the *task*. I try to do that in a way that supports the people, but for me supporting the people is supporting the people to get the task done."

"It all depends," counter two more interviewees. Dee Crabtree tries to discern whether the situation she is facing calls for holding the other in accountable partnership or providing open support for a parishioner's growth.

> There are times when I will clearly choose the task. And I will... hold somebody's toes to the fire if they haven't been doing what they needed to be doing in order for us to together have the authority to get it accomplished, and there will be other times when I will say being with So-and-so through this [hard time] and helping them grow is much more important than our getting [the job] done by such and such a date...

The choice between people and task also depends on the institutional context, observes Ruth Shinn, who finds that the Department of Labor and the First Congregational Church pull her toward different sides of the tension:

> It's my intention to do both, and the particular style will vary with the institution and the agreed-upon rules. My style of leadership when I was moderator at church was very, very different from my style at work where I am part of a hierarchy with this many people above me in the hierarchy and this many people accountable to me... Even in the hierarchical setting, which is the harder place for me to deal with authority, I try to do both, but I wouldn't be surprised but what the people I work with might say I leaned more toward the task. [And at church? As chief lay leader,] the moderator's role...is to free the group to come to its decision, and that I enjoy very much.

As a minister, Dwight Lundgren, too, sees himself as both people- and task-oriented

> ...with a priority on task-oriented. To me that's a helpful way to begin. To say "Okay, there's something that has to be accomplished." But within the context of working on that...(I'm only familiar with a church context—I haven't operated in other realms) people come to these tasks in churches with entire other agendas. They have to do with self-affirmation, and needing...I'm always very aware...of what is going on in a meeting: we've got the tasks that need to be accomplished, but we're always sensitive to why is that person saying that? What's going on in their life at this point? ...So sometimes the agenda has to go...

In church, it seems even clearer that the leader is called to attend to an integration of three dimensions: people's yearnings to make sense of their lives, the tasks of community, interpreted by the symbols of the tradition that overarch them all—in short, the individual needs, the maintenance of the community, and the tasks. This clarity in church on Sundays can usefully support the efforts of the laity in their dispersed ministries—those "harder places" to exercise authority.

Glenn Farquhar-Nicol approaches that integration from the perspective of *time*, for over time he has been learning to be not only accountable for making the most of the gift of time, but also appreciative of its graceful flow.

It depends on the situation. And I'm changing. In meetings I [once] would have been task-oriented. It can become a bit depressing if you don't achieve the task... We're changing. There are always task and people, but we're moving away from just task. In meetings now there's a minimal structure; just let it flow. I say, "God, here's a gift of time we've got together." We have to be intentional; we have a certain amount of time at our disposal.

Two more participants find that they can attend to people and task simultaneously. Peter Sherer says, "I never lose sight of the task, but very often...I see it in very people-like terms. The first task is to get a bunch of people together to do the task, then I have to divide up the responsibilities among the people..." Even though observers, watching Peter as he intuitively matches people's interests with the tasks before them, might say,

"He's concentrating on the task," people from the outside would have a hard time understanding what I'm really up to because I'm really seeing people as part of the task...assigning roles to them, monitoring them while they're doing it, in the form mostly of saying "You're terrific, keep going, you might want to do it a little more this way," if that's necessary.

I'll ask Dorothy McMahon to wind up this part of the discussion. Her comment has a paradoxical flavor, hinting not only at integration but also at the tension between people and task out of which it may be born:

I think it's the people, but as soon as I went to say that, I realized that as a minister of the Word I always have a very powerful agenda which is to keep pushing people, including myself, to understand what the mission of God might be at this moment for us. Therefore, in that sense, I need to focus on the *task*, but if it's God's task, it never subsumes the people. In fact it brings life to the people. So I guess the ultimate agenda is the people.

I invite you to join the discussion at this point. Setting your analysis in the context of recent experiences, take some time now to think about what's at stake as you consider the claims of task and people.

As you ponder your own experiences and think over the contributions all the members of our discussion group have made, notice how Integrated authority embraces the Assertive attention to task and a willingness to welcome the freedom and authority of the other people who are involved. Listen for the concern to do what's needed in the situation and the acknowledgement of contradictions transcended in a paradoxical resolution that comes as a gift, when the task can be seen in "people-like" terms, when it's clear that the task brings life to the people, when the work of the community (both the task and our experience as we address it together) feeds the yearning souls of individual members in a way that is illuminated by the symbols.

This resolution of the tension is often clearer in the church than in the secular workplace, where we must usually focus on getting the task done. Look again at Ruth Shinn's description of her two worlds on page 45 and her experience of being taken *out of the tension* in her role as church leader. Her different responsibilities as a leader in "command" and "nurture" organizations may serve to sharpen ecclesiastical ministers' appreciation of the "hard-edged" environment in which many laity do their work, and may also suggest a new slant on the church's special privilege and responsibility as "colony of heaven," holding up the "ways of home" clearly to guide those who head off to worldly workplaces on Monday morning.

Caught Between Vision and Belonging

Now we give the people/task issue a slight turn and tighten the screws with this question: "People sometimes find themselves caught between their wish to put forward a vision and their concern not to alienate the people. Do you ever get caught in that way? How do you work with that conflict?" As we explore the dilemma we can see values and issues getting clearer. We can also profit from examining what these interviewees have learned about how to manage the contradiction between those goals.

Between Vision and Belonging: the Pain

The day I talked with Colin Bradford he had just learned that he had been passed over for tenure by a major university. Piecing together his own perceptions and his conversations with colleagues, Colin concluded, "The issue basically is that I haven't conformed, and I don't do standard economics." His work was "vision-type work," but it was not seen to have the "rigor" that would come from "working in a conventional way within the discipline... Part of the reason it was being challenged was that it was...a different vision of interpretation, and it clashed directly with the conventional paradigms...The reason I wanted to regularize the appointment was really because of this tension that you mentioned, that I wanted my vision and my belonging to be congruent, and in fact they're divisive."

Colin finds his authority in his "voice." He has to speak and write the truth as he sees it even though the disjuncture between his voice and the voice of the academic establishment has brought pain and anxiety. But he is also a "people person" who holds a high value for group process and uses his voice to gather up the voices of others. He wants to evoke the authority of others in his community; but his community now refuses to authorize him. He wants to speak his mind; but by doing so he discovers he seems to have slipped to the margin of his discipline.

> Today it's very scary...I'm deathly scared...I'm walking a three-year gangplank again...I shouldn't fear being left in a vacuum or left without a job, but I *have* fears about that, and an easier way to go would be to give up the voice and belong...It's probably the shakiest moment in the entire episode...and maybe in my professional life... And it plants doubts...whether this will ever work out in a conventional academic setting of high quality, and therefore whether I shouldn't just make a decisive turn and become what I've also been in the past, which is a sort of civil servant... The safe way is to give up the unconventional analysis and become a conventional economist, which I don't think actually I am capable of being a very good one...I'm not going to abandon my views or my approach, or my philosophy, so the question really is...which institutional environment do I adapt to, an academic one or an international institutional one? And at the age of 50 that's a nontrivial choice.

In an international institution, it would "just mean less ability to speak entirely freely my own views...it requires knuckling down and doing management-style work of getting particular tasks done... This is not a question of Bradford writing down what he wants and getting it said that way, period. This is a question of an institution speaking, and...it will have to pass through lots of layers."

What matters most to Colin Bradford? When he finds himself caught between his vision and his belonging, he faces a frightening judgment call. Other interviewees, especially lay people, also spoke of finding themselves in that kind of agonizing squeeze. "The cost of exercising authority is alienation," concluded Peter Sherer.

Choices

Vision or belonging? At the moment of choice, Verna Dozier describes her experience of weighing the alternatives. Should she or should she not speak out in support of her vision?

> I have to weigh cost and promise, which is the way I talk about life in general. Is the promise I'll get for pushing my opinion, my stand now, going to be worth the alienation and separation, the image I will get of myself as being pushy? Sometimes I decide that it is and sometimes I decide it isn't, and sometimes I regret later that I didn't push, that I missed an opportunity... I have had times when I have regretted my silence when I should have said something, and there have been times when I was glad I didn't... Sometimes my reason for keeping silence is that I would lose something that I want to get, and I don't think that's a very good reason for keeping silent.

Some people, confronting such moments of choice between vision and belonging, found new possibilities emerging from a previously unexplored pole of the tension. One, whose belonging had seemed a simple given, was pressed to claim his own voice. Howard Ashby, who began by saying simply that his authority came "from God...and the people," arrived at a moment when the voice of the people and the voice of God lost their accustomed congruence and appeared to beckon him in opposite directions. Members of his vestry were saying, "You're an Anglican priest, you don't minister to all Tom, Dick, and Harry." Ashby replied, "I use my ordination service as my canons or my statutes for myself." In answer to the bishop's questions in the ordination service, he had promised to minister to "all God's people." The bishop "never said to me 'Would you just minister to Anglicans.' ...And I never had to use the canons or the statutes, I used my ordination service. The vestry wasn't happy with it but that's what I used, my authority." Ashby's Received authority thus catapulted him into Autonomy.

Others, who had begun by pushing their vision, found themselves moving alongside the people. Glenn Farquhar-Nicol said, "I've changed. I've had to acknowledge that others had visions that were at least as legitimate. A top-down attitude doesn't get anywhere. It increases people's guilt. I recognized there's another way our vision can be realized—by beginning where people are, encouraging them, awakening their hopes. It's a gentle process, recognizing them as people. A mutual process. I have to put my vision alongside theirs."

It seems reasonable to conclude that moments of choice, of being forced to wrestle with the contradiction between vision and belonging, can help people grow in authority by making them examine, entertain, and possibly expand their repertoire of options. For Howard Ashby, the contradiction pressed him toward greater Autonomy. For Glenn Farquhar-Nicol, "weighing cost and promise" under judgment led him toward Integrated values of respect for others' freedom and authority.

Living Between Vision and Belonging in Community

Finding themselves torn between their vision for what might be and the complexities of a social system that does not share that vision, lay people have learned to accept small incremental gains. In Ruth Shinn's well-seasoned reflection on her work in the Department of Labor, she acknowledges

> times when my vision is different from my superior's, but I know that...their boss won the election and under our system they have the right to pursue the policies they're pursuing, and I recognize that, and so I give input and technical support and everything that I reasonably can in the direction of what I want to do, but if they want to

do something different I have to prepare support material for that.
I've thought that one through very carefully, and I can live with
that, because I do believe in a two-party system... And sometimes
you nudge things, and sometimes you improve things along the
way. I think you can make incremental differences, and so that's
one reason I stay inside the system...

For some of the clergy, the truest vision arises *out of* their community. Susan Adams believes that often "maintenance of the community
of faith that you're part of or the community of people that you're working on behalf of...becomes more important than spinning off by yourself
into a realm of vision that nobody else is able to recognize or grasp."
She sees herself as carrying authority from the women's movement to
the several male-dominated boards and committees on which she sits: "I
say my piece there but I say it out of the strength of the women's movement." In her concern to develop the ministry of the laity in Colchester
Church, Dee Crabtree "instinctively knew" that the mission groups used
by other churches "wouldn't work in Colchester, and that to address the
lives of the people there, part of what I needed to do was help them discover the authority of their own lives and the possible ministries that they
might have,...introducing the ministry of the laity in such a way that it...
would fit with their culture..." Similarly Jim Adams has come to reject
goals as the driving force for ministry; when he gets attached to goals, "it
just causes trouble." I summarized his comments in these words: "That's
not the center of it for you. The point is not getting x, y, or z done, it's
how we're living here." Adams replied, "Yes, it really is."
    Even in the community's *resistance* to the vision, Dorothy McMahon
sees herself as a participant. She reflects on times

when I've had a clear and painful sense that the word that's being
addressed to us is not one we want to hear. I've usually found that
if I put it in those terms, the people will struggle with it. That it's
the word *we* don't want to hear. If I say *they* don't want to hear, or
you don't want to hear, then I find that it's really hard to move
forward. But if I can authentically say "I too sit under this" (and I
usually can because it's usually something that has been hard-won
by me as the Word)...it is with some pain and fear that I put it out in
front of us. I also think that some of our best moments in parish life

> have been when we think something has been asked of us from
> outside and we have had the guts to say to each other, "We can't
> cope, so we'll have to say no," and confess that... For a body of
> Christians corporately to say this is to prepare the ground... I've
> been taught by God through my spiritual director to be gentle with
> myself and to enter the feelings that I have when something is asked
> of me that I don't want to do, and the gracious and grieving pro-
> cesses that you go through with a group of people are the same as
> the processes that you go through with yourself before God...

Where vision and human community meet, we may experience a paradoxical range of pain and possibility. We may, like Colin Bradford, find
ourselves in an agonizing squeeze between the need to follow a calling
and the need to be affirmed by our belonging. We may, with Verna
Dozier, face difficult choices whose rightness is so much clearer in retro-
spect than at the moment when our decision is required. The squeeze
may press us toward growth in Autonomy, as it did for Howard Ashby.
Or, like Glenn Farquhar-Nicol, we may find ourselves pushed beyond the
boundaries of our personal Assertiveness. We may join Ruth Shinn in a
patient, watchful coexistence with the powers that be, and an increasing
comfort with small steps forward. With Susan Adams and Dee Crabtree,
we may come to see our vision itself as rooted in the community of faith.
We may join Jim Adams in the discovery that our own truest vision is
most fully expressed, not in the struggle over specific advocacies, but in
how we're living here in our church. With Dorothy McMahon, we might
see the contradiction between me-as-the-person-with-the-vision and
those-resistant-people overcome in our sense of solidarity with the community—even when it says "No" to the vision—and come to acknowledge that "the tension between vision and belonging is within me." The
collision between vision and belonging contains all that struggle—and all
those redemptive possibilities.

*For your reflection: As you think about the places in your life where you
want to follow a vision and where you also yearn to belong, where is the
pain and where are the hints of resurrection for you now?*

When My Authority Is Challenged

Sometimes wrenching conflict arises not only inside us but also between us and the people who have asked us to exercise authority on their behalf. I asked Joyce Yarrow to tell me about a time when her authority was challenged.

> The experience that brought me most pain, and also most growth, was the first three years after I took over as Executive Director of the Hartford Region YWCA back in 1979. We were trying very hard to deal with racism and sexism. The YWCA was going through some real pain on account of those issues, because we had black and Hispanic women, some radical lesbian women as well as some middle and upper class straight women. There were some very personal and painful issues for people to deal with. At the same time we had a very large agency, about the tenth largest YWCA in the country, that was going through some severe financial troubles and almost went bankrupt... Some real vengeance being expressed.
>
> And I'm the leader. I'm the new executive. I'm white. Everybody wanted those problems solved overnight. And I was pressed to present plans and actions that would make those problems go away—immediately.
>
> At the same time, the board reorganization plan that the executive committee and I worked out with the board meant that all forty-five members of the board would resign so they could re-seat a board of twenty-four. We would have a more manageable board for management purposes, as well as a more diverse board. We ended up with a board that was a third black, a third Hispanic, and a third other, instead of a board that numbered forty-five with only five black women and the rest white women, most of whom did not work.
>
> Remember that I'm the white executive in this scenario. I was the pivot person who understood the purpose of these severe structural changes. I was also the person being attacked by people who had lost their power or their authority. And I was dealing with this situation in the midst of enormous internal cultural, racial, and lifestyle diversity and major external change.
>
> It was the most painful experience of my life. People were acting

out their confusion and frustration on my position as executive and on me as the person in that position. Sometimes the acting out was only because I had the authority. And other times it was because I was different from them. Or because they wanted me to do my job differently. When the board started to act out on the staff, I was accused of everything you can think of. At the same time my best friend had just died of alcoholism.

So the crux of it for me was that my personal and professional standards were being challenged. My integrity was being challenged. My competence was being challenged. It would have been easy to say "It's not worth it" and walk away from that situation. It took a severe toll on me personally, professionally, and spiritually.

I asked: "What could sustain you at a time like that?" Joyce replied:

I ended up in therapy and that was one of the things that helped me make it through that time. Some very close friends helped me through that time, and also trying to work through to a greater faith or spirituality.

I lived through it. And I lived through it to regain the control of who I was, to rebuild my personal and professional self-confidence and self-esteem, and to work with the board and staff to turn the agency around so that we ended up with a positive balance for five years...I left that agency eight years later in a very safe and secure and stable place, having been affirmed as a good manager who was sensitive to multicultural issues, and having made some very dear black and Hispanic friends who have helped me move on to form this organization.

That whole experience gave me the knowledge and strength to serve as a consultant and trainer with other organizations and executives who are struggling with those very same issues. And I have developed some models and some ways of working so that hopefully it won't be as painful for them as it was for me.

Joyce Yarrow's story reminds me of a painting of a storm—a gale of social forces and emergent meanings that brought Joyce to the very edge of her resources. In this big picture we see clearly that the integration of person and context in authority has not only a promising but also an agonizing side. The challenge to authority becomes a challenge to the totality of a person. The requirement: to stand. To "live through" the storm is to have gained strength to offer to others.

We will follow this large canvas of a storm with some smaller "detail" pictures of challenge to authority that may help us examine some themes from the gale: the nature of the crunch, the leader's responses to challenge, the shape of resurrection, and the sources of sustenance.

The Nature of the Crunch

Where is "the eye of the storm" when your authority is challenged? Where is the real crux of the matter?

"I would say my authority was challenged every single time I opened my mouth," recalled Dee Crabtree as she thought back years ago to the time when she first spoke out on women's issues in the U.C.C. "What is at stake for you in such challenges?" I asked. Listen to this capable, intelligent woman's response: "It will often cause me to question my own intellectual ability...'Oh, maybe I really am stupid'... I just dispense with my authority. I just basically say, 'Oh, well of course he knows what he is talking about. And I have to really maintain strong discipline in myself to bring myself to speak up in those situations where my view is different..." What's at stake? "Identity and security," replied Dee.

A couple of interviewees noticed that the challenge to their identity and security was more intense in a family setting than it was at work. When students confront her, "It feels fine," said Judith McMorland. It feels dreadful when her son challenges her.

Others pointed out how the level of stress gets turned up when the challenge is embedded in a broader conflict. "We huddle together," said Keith Mason of his colleagues in the struggle for the ordination of women. In conflicted systems people's identity and security are massively threatened, and they find it much more difficult to exercise their authority easily and flexibly on their own.

Challenge embedded in conflict throws our need to belong and our need to have a point of view, our security and our identity, into a very shaky place. At bottom, concluded Peter Sherer, the issue beneath all those is "Who am I?" "The longer [the challenge] goes on the deeper the distrust of myself and my gift... And if I'm not that package of gifts, *who am I?*"

How Leaders Respond to Challenge

When leaders' identity and security are shaken by challenge, what useful responses have they discovered? Two interviewees' answers illustrated the double demand they faced: Hear where the challenge is coming from and don't let yourself get pushed over. Dwight Lundgren told how he was standing at the church door shaking hands after the service when an older woman came up to him. "She was trembling, and suddenly she just starts reaming me out. 'The church is falling apart. It's all your fault.'" Dwight drove to the head deacon's house. He said, "'I really need to talk to you about this'... I quickly realized she had just over the past year gone through retirement. And everything that had held together for her was coming apart, and she just needed someone to unload on... The energy that she was bringing to it...was garnered from a lot of different things going on. And that was a very helpful thing for me to reflect on." He needed *to hear where the challenge was coming from.*

Glenn Farquhar-Nicol told of his struggle with parishioners who had responsible positions in their workplace, but went into a state of collapse in the church. "They continually wanted me to treat them as children and be the authority for them: 'Tell us exactly what you want us to do.' In a sense my authority was challenged because they wanted to impose a view of authority on me that was not mine, without thinking about it...I resisted strongly." Glenn knew he had not only to listen to where the challenge was coming from but also, for the sake of their growth as well as his own authenticity, to *resist the temptation to capitulate.*

Fear can keep me from listening and from standing firm, from being with *what is* and from being who *I am.* Each of us needs to find ways to manage our fear. In the midst of that stress, sometimes I can just let it be that I am scared, and go ahead and do what I have to do. Acknowledging my vulnerability to myself and in God can give me strength to face the challenges from without.

As Keith Mason reflected on homely challenges like that of the five-year-old who refuses to get into the bath, he said, "One of the lessons my wife and I have tried to teach each other is not to make too much of an issue over certain things because the danger is always that the ultimate issue becomes your authority rather than the task at hand or the long-term happiness of the unit or of the child." The issue easily becomes "Who's in charge?" when that is not what is at stake. People who exercise Integrated authority focus on doing what's needed and hold their authority lightly. This lightness seems to be less difficult for some of the older interviewees, who seem to have settled into an easier stance toward challenges over the years.

Hearing others voice their truth, standing firm in one's own truth, holding (but not grasping) authority to do what's needed—those are the ways these leaders respond to challenge in a manner designed to serve their people.

The Shape of Resurrection

Even when challenge brings agony as intense as Joyce Yarrow's, our interviewees are hopeful that good things can emerge at the end of the storm. Many of these leaders, especially the older ones, articulate their concern about how the encounter might benefit the people who are challenging them. As he told the story of the recently retired woman who "reamed him out," Lundgren reflected empathically on the meaning of the attack for her.

Dorothy McMahon, too, reflected on times of challenge as "good encounters":

I have had challenges to my authority in the parish, in spite of all my wonderful ideals I've just put in front of you, when sometimes I do just go blazing in. I'm an enthusiast and I'm an ideas person so I just go *Hah*! into a meeting, and then I have had parishioners or parish councillors or elders say, "Hey, just a minute! You're being pretty heavy here! How can we participate in this decision when you are putting such pressure on us?" I have had times when I've put up an idea and people have said, "No, we don't think that is a good idea at all, and are you really listening?" I have responded very defensively sometimes and I have responded with hurt. And I've had to be challenged about those responses, too. Because people respect what I normally do, they find it very hard to challenge me at all, and they are afraid that I might withdraw my approval and love from them. So we've had some quite good encounters with each other...

All these clergy were willing to do what Jack Harris held was necessary: "to expose themselves to the ultimate weapon of a voluntary association—the power to criticize, withdraw, and neutralize the authority of the leader."[1] Those who exercise Integrated authority do not clutch it anxiously, but willingly put it at risk, as they seek to follow One whose surrender of control proved to be, at the story's end, the opening toward resurrection.

Sources of Sustenance

What sustains you in the face of challenge? In spite of her frustration, said Ruth Shinn, one of the older interviewees, "I don't feel totally undermined by it... I don't feel anything that anybody has thrown at me really ever gets all the way to the core...I can't think of any time anybody has touched my own center of worth. There's a given there... My center of worth doesn't depend on these things that come and go." Glenn Farquhar-Nicol, the youngest interviewee, was finding ways to sustain that "center of worth" that one of the eldest found at her core. Said Glenn, "I spend a half hour in silence at the beginning of each day. During time with God, with significant others, my worth is not at risk. I spend that time on angers and hurts so I don't have ongoing conflicts. Therefore I can go back and talk with them and be more objective. I'm more in touch with why. I don't feel threatened in the same way then."

The oldest interviewee, Verna Dozier, remembering herself as an "authoritative" young woman, has come to a seasoned certainty: "I really *do* believe that we are not saved by the rightness of our answer or the rightness of our stance."

Another younger interviewee, Peter Sherer, finds ways to counteract the distrust of himself and his gifts that challenges engender: "Friends. The knowledge that life isn't easy, the thought that this, too, will pass. I pray and put myself in churchy circumstances [where] I'm reminded that I might not be running the railroad by myself... The only thing God expects me to do is keep putting one foot in front of the other."

These leaders draw a coherent picture of Integrated authority in the face
of challenge. The challenge is this: finding a way to stand, rooted in
one's center, while acknowledging the authority of others. The willingness to open oneself to struggle, to try simply to do what's needed,
means that at the end—in spite of the pain—it is often possible to call
these challenges "good encounters." The older ones stand: "I am not
destroyed." "My center of worth doesn't depend on these things that
come and go." And the younger ones find ways to support and replenish
their center.

A question for reflection: What ways have you discovered to support and
nourish your center of worth in the face of challenge?

Promise and Problems in Roles

I asked interviewees: "Is your authority dependent on or independent of
a role?" When we remember that this group of leaders set more store on
inner than *given* authority, we won't be surprised to find most of them
saying their authority is independent of the roles they occupy. Peter
Sherer replies: "Independent. I bring my authority to the roles I play
and invest the role with the authority." Judith McMorland agrees: "I
find myself within situations where I'm seen to be authoritative regardless of what the context is."

Several, particularly clergywomen, would agree with Dee Crabtree's
statement: "Often for *others* my role as the senior minister of the church
carries with it a kind of authority, particularly on Sunday mornings. But
for me my authority is not connected to that role..." It is useful to note
here that those who look at the authority figure from the outside are not
well positioned to distinguish person and role and find it natural to focus
on the role. In the same way those who look at authority through a
sociological lens naturally concentrate on authority in role. Looking at
her authority from the inside, Dee Crabtree has a vantage point from
which she can discriminate between herself and her role. She perceives
these two realities as having a tensive relationship.

Ruth Shinn captured a different truth: "[My authority] is through a
role because I said it was very different as moderator in a church from
team leader." Looking at two different experiences of exercising authority, Ruth sees that the role *shapes* her authority.

Roles have the power to shape our authority. Yet many of us hesitate to ascribe major importance to our roles. Let's pursue this ambivalence further by assessing the cost and promise of the roles we play.

What do roles cost us?

Interviewees find many reasons to make negative judgments about roles. While Susan Adams acknowledges that she has institutional authority in her role as parish priest, she concludes, "I don't think that authority for me is as important as the other, which seems to me to be more genuine and have more power to energize and move people to it than an exercise of institutional power that comes with a role or an office." Colin Bradford, for whom authority is "my voice," voices suspicion of the power of roles because they inhibit life. His worst job experience was in "a pre-existing slot." He remarks, "I do better in unstructured places where I'm creating the form rather than when I'm meant to fit the form." Dorothy McMahon, with her high value for the *human*, sees authority arising from people's recognizing "truth in a person." When her parishioners assume that her authority comes from a role, she says, "I tend to deal with it by trying to establish a very human relationship with the people that I'm working with so that real authority has a chance of breaking through instead of superficial authority... In a hierarchical relationship with people, you don't have any real relationship with them. It's not something that feels good in my view, and therefore if I have to be in a role, I am alienated and separated from people and I feel very lonely."

Roles can't give leaders competence or creativity, and they get in the way of life-giving human connections. But roles may have more distinctly negative effects. Lay men articulate the clearest awareness of how their activities in role have the possibility of doing harm to other people—especially in "command" (as opposed to "nurture") organizations, where executives may be pushed to sacrifice the needs of individuals to the requirements of the bottom line.

When these leaders make negative judgments about the power of role, they seem to be rejecting role as hierarchy—control and ranking—rather than role as a functional description of responsibilities. When they think of role as defining *responsibility*, they evaluate it positively.

The Promise of Roles

Glenn Farquhar-Nicol, who said the clearest "no" to role as control and ranking, also said the clearest "yes" to role as function and responsibility. "My role and others' roles are worked out clearly. We know who's responsible for what. We have clear functions." Clergy who are clear about their role and responsibilities are perceived as having authority, as Loma Balfour affirmed: "I see authority very closely tied to responsibility, and you can't have one without the other..."

A role gives a leader permission to *take* authority. Jim Adams, looking ahead to retirement, imagined that it would be hard no longer to have a "place of authority," "a structural position in which you speak and get heard. I think it will be hard for me not to have the parish..." Keith Mason, too, acknowledged that his role as Queen's Counsel enhanced his ability to speak and be heard. The morning of our interview, said Keith, "When my junior barrister, who is older than me and whom I regard as wiser than me within his particular area, didn't think much of what I said in court this morning, he whispered to me, 'You know, if a junior barrister says that, it's rubbish; if a Q.C. says that it's still rubbish, but they listen.'"

Roles provide those who inhabit them with useful power; but interviewees also say that their roles place *limits* upon them in ways that are beneficial to the people they serve. "If I see myself as a participant in the group with no responsibility for the group's functioning in any overt sense, then I would feel free to participate and speak," says Susan Adams. But "if I'm there as the group facilitator, then obviously my opinion can wait." I find leading always requires that I put limits on myself for the sake of the group. If I want to evoke the contributions of others, I have to set my personal agenda aside and loosen control. The role of leader helps me to focus on what the people need done; the role leads me to work at being helpful to whoever is present—even people who might not appeal to me if I met them at a party. Jackson Carroll helpfully describes the character of role as "schoolmaster," guiding us toward fulfilling the responsibilities of the role even when our personal motivation for doing so flags.[2]

Our interviewees' ambivalence about role suggests that we appreciate the paradoxical nature of roles. Roles give people power to serve; roles also help people serve by placing limitations on them. This paradox might again remind us that it is the One who "knew that the Father had put everything into his hands" who "tied a towel around himself" and "poured water into a basin and began to wash the disciples' feet..." (Jn. 13:3-4) Role as control and ranking is thus replaced by role as responsibility expressed in both power and obedience. A role is useful not when it sets the leader over others as one who controls, but when it helps the leader be responsible as one who serves. John Howard Yoder says it well: "The notion that God himself has renounced rule for servanthood and calls us to do the same (Phil. 2:5-11) is paradoxically a powerful thought."[3]

I but not I

From the inner perspective of the person living with authority, Dwight Lundgren has this to say: "To me it's very important to keep my identity clear from the role. I'm more than a minister and I'm also less than a minister." The paradox becomes visible when he is "putting the robe on, putting the vestments on. Something very deep and profound as well as something very mundane happens when you do that... When I put the robe on it, at one level, represents the skills"—seminary training and expertise. "But there is also the sense of 'I am I but not I' when I do that, but I'm trying to tell people...that we're all fools for Christ. This is kind of a game we're playing. So we're to take it seriously, but not too seriously... If we remember this as a game, kind of like a dance, then we won't get into trouble."

Our generation is presented with a fresh possibility for living in the tension between person and role, accepting the paradoxical "I but not I" character of living with authority. As institutional clarity about and support for our traditional roles wore thin, we were forced to shape our roles in a more personal way. Because we lost the consensus about our roles that once seemed self-evident, parents have had to decide what kind of parents they want to be, clergy to customcraft their role as religious leaders. Many of us have *had* to struggle free of being collapsed into our roles—for our souls' sake. At one point Joyce Yarrow realized to her chagrin that she had so *become* her role "that if I lost my job I felt I would have lost my life..." Now she has learned "that my self and my authority comes from me, not the position I hold... My gifts...go with me no matter where I am." Joyce had to distinguish her life from her role.

Many of us have found promise in rediscovering the person side of person-in-role; we can shape our roles more creatively and be more authentically ourselves within them. The more recent temptation has been to flop to the other side of the tension, emphasizing our individuality and looking down on roles. Having experienced these extremes within our memory, we may be better able to accept the claim of both poles of the tension and avoid settling for either as simply "the answer." Each of us may then be able to consent to live with the struggle entailed in knowing that *I am me* and knowing also that *I am a responsible part of this social system.* Joyce Yarrow speaks from that Integrated, paradoxical place:

> Sometimes the authority or the power that is viewed as only the title of the position or the role that you're in at the time...[is] what people interact [with] and react to. And oftentimes you are speaking more in a personal way from that position and giving your own opinion, not necessarily the opinion of the position...[It's a] risk. And...if you can take...the time...to weigh the risk and the consequence, and is it what the group needs to do?... Is it what you're being called to do? And to do the best you can at the time you're doing it with the information you do have, and be willing to say "I'm sorry" or "I shouldn't have done that," or "I wish I had done it differently but that's what I did at the time."

Several interviewees offer suggestions for how we might faithfully live in the balance required of the person-in-role, the one who is "I but not I." Keith Mason models the lightness that is required, the willingness not to take oneself overly seriously: "If a Q.C. says that it's still rubbish, but they listen." Mason also shows an awareness that a role requires more than one person's gifts; for that reason, he says: "I never get caught in selecting my successor." His perception that the role transcends the person provides a counterpoint to Joyce Yarrow's learning that the person transcends the role. Dorothy McMahon teases role and person apart by making it a habit to move in and out of role; to do so underlines the functional instead of the hierarchical nature of the pastor's job and gives lay people opportunities to exercise their own authority as leaders. Like Dorothy McMahon, Susan Adams tries "to occupy these roles in a way which is human, and is not authoritarian." A human way of exercising authority softens the contradiction between person and role.

These leaders also consent to live in the contradiction between their own view from within and the perceptions of others that come to them from without. On one hand Dee Crabtree claims her own inner conviction that her authority does not reside primarily in the role of senior minister; on the other hand she is willing to remind herself of the importance of that role to others and to behave accordingly. Holding these two truths together is an important part of the integration between her inner reality and the context in which she lives and works. The internal perspective into which these leaders invite us may thus illuminate the challenge of Integrated authority: to inhabit the role, to differentiate oneself, and to accept the task of living in the tension between role and selfhood.

Before we move more deeply into an examination of how leaders live in that tension, take a little time to reflect on your own experience with your role.

Do you find your authority dependent on or independent of a role?

What is the promise and what is the cost of your role? Reflect on your experience and make two lists.

Where do you get clarity and support for living in the contradiction between your own inner perception of your leadership and what you can gather about the perceptions of others?

Have you experienced roles as paradoxical? If so, how?

Can you think of any religious symbols that illuminate that paradox powerfully for you?

Fielding Other People's Projections

> And the man [Paul healed] sprang up and began to walk. When the crowds saw what Paul had done, they shouted in the Lycaonian language, "The gods have come down to us in human form!" ...When the apostles Barnabas and Paul heard of it, they tore their clothes and rushed out into the crowd, shouting, "Friends, why are you doing this? We are mortals just like you..."(Acts 14:10-11, 14-15)

"Why are you doing this?" The Religious Meaning of Projection

What's going on when we begin to feel like a movie screen on which pictures from an alien projector are flickering? Where are the pictures coming from? How can we respond to them in a way that's true to ourselves and helpful to others?

If we are going to be able to deal in a useful way with the disjuncture between our own picture of ourselves and others' pictures of us, we need to have both pictures accessible to us. Here we need to include within our framework an awareness of others as subject (the projector) and ourselves as object (the screen).

Projections reveal people's longings for an authority figure who is unfailingly strong and caring and who will, at the same time, allow them to be free. But in the end nobody seems to be able to fulfil those yearnings completely: neither parents, nor teachers, nor the subsequent authority figures to whom people bring those ancient hopes.

We are tempted here to focus on the screen; but it will be more useful to try to discern what's going on in the projector—the source of the pictures in human hopes and disappointments. Richard Sennett has analyzed people's ways of living with the dilemma that they want more from authority figures than those figures can deliver. He describes people's jerry-built schemes for living in this often unbearable conflict: "I need one who will be strong and care for me, while preserving my freedom, and you might be the one. But I know, or fear, that you aren't powerful enough, that you don't love me as much as I need to be loved—or, even if you could be powerful and loving, that I could not preserve my own selfhood in the face of all you provide."

The first scheme Sennett outlines is *disobedient dependence*. He tells the story of a young woman who, by dating men of whom her parents strongly disapprove, succeeds in feeling comfortable enough to spend relaxed weekends at home with mom and dad. She is not rebelling *against* authority; that would leave her free to marry one of the men or leave the city. Instead she is rebelling *within* authority: her parents' wishes provide the whole context in which she lives her life.[4]

The second scheme is *idealized substitution*. The boss provides a negative model of authority; employees inwardly protest: "If only there were someone different in control! Whatever you are is the opposite of the authority I want." While this strategy allows the employee to steal an illusion of independence, his picture is like a photographic negative: the fact that the ideal is defined as "not you" means that "it is your image I am always printing."[5]

The third scheme for living in the tension between longings and reality is *fantasized disappearance.* "Everything would be all right if only the people in charge would disappear." But if they did disappear, the subject would feel abandoned. Here is one more way to have rebellion and security at the same time, if only in a carefully constructed make-believe world. Through these strategies, says Sennett, people can protest the inadequacy of the authority and assert their wish to be free without running the terrifying risk of actually cutting loose from their moorings and sailing off on their own.

An analysis like Sennett's may help those exercising authority make sense of some baffling and distressing behavior on the part of the people they are trying to work with. Knowing, with Paul and Barnabas, that "we are mortals just like you," leaders can work to help people move past their conflicted worship toward a recognition that all human authority is finite. The projectors can then lay aside their limping schemes and direct their hunger for a caring and freedom-giving power toward God, claim for themselves their own appropriate measure of authority, and, realizing that the authority figure they have cast as the protagonist in their inner drama is only human, turn their attention to their own responsibilities.

This discovery that perfect authority belongs only to God makes possible a degree of realism that benefits both parties in this drama. Our spiritual hunger is the truth about us, and until we recognize it for what it is we will distort our own reality and that of others. By working to reveal this truth, authority figures will gain the satisfaction of helping others grow spiritually. They will also gain relief from the burden of unrealistic demands and they will be better equipped to handle the pain of being attacked whenever their clay feet are revealed.

Leaders who hear the religious question hidden in projection can make some sense of the resentment, irritation, anger, even rage that come their way when the projectors' hopes go unfulfilled. When teaching classes for new members, Jim Adams found "people really want me and my colleagues to straighten them out spiritually. When we don't, they become irritated..." Dwight Lundgren had learned through experience that those whose admiration for the pastor knows no bounds "can, in the flick of an eye, also blame you incommensurably." We prop our authority figures on the pedestal of our hopes; when they fail us, we tear them down in our rage.

Understanding projection helps leaders make sense of those attacks;

their understanding also equips them to help others resolve the problems and reach for the promise hidden in the process of playing their inner longings out on an external screen. As Jim Adams put it, "People don't work on their own authority until they are willing to withdraw what they are inappropriately projecting onto me." Parishioners can get very busy with the institutional life of their church and their clergy in a way that keeps their energies from being released for the real and pressing battles with which their lives confront them. Jesus countered the preoccupation that fastened upon him ("Blessed is the womb that bore you") by pointing people out toward their responsibilities ("Blessed rather are those who hear the word of God and obey it!") Lk. 11:27-28.

Even though projecting means *displacing* our truth, that process of displacement can be illuminating: when our inner pictures are out there flickering on the screen *we can see them.* The most profound truths about our lives, after all, are accessible only in symbolic form—individuals' dreams and images and our corporate myths and symbols. Once we see those "mythic contents" on the screen, says Walter Wink, our next "task is simply to complete the circle by an interpretation that finds their meaning back in the one and only real world..." [6]

The authority figure is strategically placed to assist people in that task. Accepting our role as a symbol for others, we as authority figures must point beyond ourselves (that's what all symbols do) to the true source of all authority. The authority's task is reminiscent of that wonderful painting by Leonardo da Vinci in which the infant John the Baptist points his finger toward the Christ child. Or Jesus' answer when the devil seductively laid out kingdoms before him: "It is written, 'Worship the Lord your God, and serve only him.'" (Lk. 4: 5-8) When people come to the leader asking for the truth about their lives, the Integrated leader finds a way to protest: "Don't look to me, I can't give it to you; but join me in the search." With Paul and Barnabas, the leader replies: "Why are you doing this? We are mortals just like you, and we bring you good news, that you should turn...to the living God..."

Managing projections means letting the others in on that truth. And people with Integrated authority seem equipped to understand and convey it. In their responses to others, they can say, "All authority belongs to God. Here are the boundaries between you and me and God, as I see them. I invite you, too, to exercise your authority under God." People with Integrated authority have gotten clearer about what's within them and what's out there in the world around them and can be helpful to others who also seek such clarity.

How the Interviewees Manage Projections

Out of their experience with a highly symbolic role, clergy immediately responded to the question about projection, recounting situations and describing their strategy. Lay people often worked briefly to connect the question with their experiences and then replied with stories and strategies.

Peter Sherer and Jim Adams acknowledged that projections were useful as a first step. Said Peter, "If it's early in the process that's very useful for me. It's required for people to load me up with authority early in the process because I have to overcome inertia. Later on it is counter-productive because the only way to sustain real change is to have people buy into the process." Jim Adams allowed that "the perception of divine authority draws people to me. Then to gain anything useful we have got to put it aside...I try to use the perception of divine authority responsibly, and give people their religious authority back."

Projections test leaders' ability to define themselves, just as challenges from others do. The question is, "How do you maintain your Autonomous authority in the face of seduction and attack?" Attacks face us with a test: "Will you maintain your own sense of your authority?" Seduction raises the additional question, "Do you care whether others maintain *their* authority?" Both challenge the leader to learn to sit loose to the judgments of this world. As soon as religious leaders unquestioningly accept the admiration seductively laid out before them they have forfeited their authenticity.

The leader needs to discern: *What appropriately belongs to me?* Ruth Shinn provided a glimpse into her process of discernment as she looked at the pictures beamed in her direction and sorted out which she would accept: "Just recently, and this is a new role, I think I've come to an age where some of the women...are beginning to attribute the sage role to me, and they want me to accept it. They want me to enjoy the fact that they enjoy me, and so I've been sort of feeling my way into trying to be graceful about that without wanting to take on the notion of being more of a sage than I am."

Peter Sherer, too, tested the pictures: "Inappropriate admiration is always a red flag and I notice it. It causes me to ask 'Am I creating a fan club or solving a problem?'" Other interviewees often concluded this inner sorting process with the decision: *"I'm not going to take it."* It was clear to Joyce Yarrow that her nonprofit executive clients should feel proud of their success in learning more effective leadership styles. While she may have offered them some new ideas, they had to "practice and experience to make it theirs. Once they make it theirs *they* have made the growth experience. It wasn't mine to do for them." Therefore, *"they should take the credit* and not give the credit to me." Several other leaders refused to take the responsibility they had determined belonged properly to others. Throwing it "back in their court," Glenn Farquhar-Nicol tells parishioners, "'You're an adult; you need to make a decision.'

These leaders had thought through some strategies for communicating clearly to others their determination not to coopt the authority, responsibility, or applause that belonged to others. Ruth Shinn emphasized the light touch.

> When a group of people project on you more omniscience or wisdom than you have, one of the things I do is simply to say, Hey, look, I make mistakes, don't count on it. And sometimes I make jokes about myself, just to ease things a little. Because I am knowledgeable in my field, there's no question about it, but I don't want to take myself too seriously."

Peter Sherer had a strategy for responding to excessive admiration when it came his way in sexual guise: "Advances I feel from women or men—covert sexual advances—I usually ignore. I pretend I'm not getting the message though it's clear as a bell."

Dorothy McMahon said "I'm not going to take it" through a well-rounded strategy for undermining parishioners' inappropriate dependence on her:

> I go into the Parish Council and I say, "Well, I messed that one up, didn't I?" And they say, "Yes, you did."...I reinforce people's awareness that they're not actually dependent on my presence...But I also try to share honestly with some members of the congregation, particularly the Elders' Council, what is happening for me in my

own spiritual pilgrimage. Now I know that parishes can't cope with
a "breaking down" minister—one who is really disintegrating—but
they can, in fact, cope with a person who is acknowledging very
deep levels of humanness.

Interviewees found ways to say not only *"I'm not going to take it,"*
speaking out of their Autonomous authority, but also an Assertive *"You
take it!"* reminiscent of Jesus redirecting his hearers' attention: "Blessed
rather are those who hear the word of God and obey it!" When she perceived people abdicating their authority, Verna Dozier often immediately identified what she saw: "I try to name it, and then I might say to the
person, 'I think you've just given away your authority.' Sometimes
people understand that and sometimes they don't. And then I say to
people what I...say so often, 'You are worthy, and you are precious. Just
claim that!'" Responding to students who think he is "knowledgeable on
absolutely everything," Colin Bradford turns "the question back on the
student...'You're really not asking a question; you're making an assertion. What do you think?'" Susan Adams used Letty Russell's idea of
"planned inefficiency" in church committee work—"actually deliberately
being unable, unavailable, or messing up something in order that the person or people or group will pick it up again because you're unable to do
it satisfactorily... 'Oh I can't *possibly* do that'...because I actually think
the treasurer should work it out or the accountant and not *me*."

Our leaders also found ways to tell people: *"Give it to God."*
"Don't look to me as the ultimate source of authority; that source is
transcendent." Howard Ashby articulated this clearly: "They say how
you've done good for them...I always tell them, 'Don't give the glory to
me, give it to God.'"

The management of projections requires Integrated authority. The
projections may be initially granted because of Received authority. The
designated authority attracts and crystalizes people's deep longings for
dependable care. Then the authority figure needs Autonomous authority
to tease the transcendent hopes apart from the personal realities of the
projector and the screen. Assertive authority is required for the interven-
tion: *"You take it,"* or *"Give it to God."* Without Integrated authority,
the leader lacks the overall perspective to carry out this complex task,
and is instead tempted to own transcendent projections as personal pro-
perty and gobble up ego gratification, to reject the person who comes

with the projections, or to miss opportunities for speaking the truth and inviting people to inherit the authority that is theirs. For leaders with Integrated authority, projections present a powerful opportunity to proclaim the conviction that all authority comes from God.

Questions for reflection: Think of a time when someone else presented you with an unfamiliar picture of reality, one that seemed foreign because you were seen as a powerful source of good or evil. What might have been going on? How did you respond? What was useful about your response and how could it have been more helpful?

CHAPTER IV

Authority in Different Voices

Loma Balfour brightened as she remembered telling her husband that she couldn't keep on looking to him as a model for being a priest: "Look, darling, it's no use. I'm not you, and I can't do it that way." Glenn Farquhar-Nicol remembered a different turning in the path: "My early authoritarian view was not positive...I changed from a dragging mode to an encouraging mode." Having sketched *generic* patterns of growth in authority in Chapter 2, let's go back and listen to the different accents and cadences of women and men as they describe their journeys toward Integrated authority. As we look at female and male tendencies, remember that the path you are treading is uniquely yours, and notice where your way is like or unlike the generalized descriptions in this chapter. *As you read these descriptions, highlight or underline what describes your experience.*

A Woman's Way

Women often sparkled with energy as they answered my question: "Do you find any special strength or difficulty in dealing with your authority because you are a woman?" Judith McMorland spoke of how her male students, having come to her perhaps about a teaching matter, now opened up to her about their spiritual experience "...acknowledging the wholeness of their lives." "I will evoke that as part of my relationship with them," she reflected. Then she looked back a bit ruefully: "I've given my power away all the time... I used to think that some of these men were much more powerful; now I'm feeling much more confident that actually there isn't anybody I couldn't talk to, peer to peer." As a child she had been imbued with "the sense that the church was quite hierarchical, so there was GOD, and there was Daddy, and there was us. That picture takes a very long time to get into perspective." Fairly recently, the picture has shifted as Judith has come to own her own authority and to know from the inside who she is. "How has that happened?" I asked. "I think it is that point of transition of having confronted the authority figures and come to that point of readiness to take one's own authority," she replied.

Receiving Woman

Like many women, Judith McMorland reviews several chapters of the story of her growth in authority with interest and excitement. As they look back to the beginning of the story in Received authority, women typically remember themselves in a receptive posture toward the authority exercised by men, unlike their brothers, who had often received authority roles ready made. In their personal lives, some of these women spent their twenties postponing the claiming of their own identity while they received it vicariously through a male partner's achievements. If we back away and look at the whole culture, we see many men and women in the Received stage joined in a symbiotic relationship: he exercises authority as he has received it, while she receives his authority. ("There was GOD, and there was Daddy, and there was us.") There is promise in this arrangement, for each is in touch with a piece of the whole reality of authority, but there is also a problem, for whatever comfort women and men derive from their mutual accommodation is purchased at the cost of their wholeness.

Women in this stage are laying a foundation that may serve them well in the future, for a Receptive posture toward the authority of God and the authority of other people is an essential ingredient in Integrated authority. In the experiential courses on authority from which the interview questions were drawn, our first step was to tell stories about important early authority figures and to explore their impact on our own growth in authority—an impact people described as movingly powerful and pervasive. Acknowledging what we have received is an important foundation; but we have some building to do before it becomes authority.

A woman in the Receiving stage experiences significant problems. Chief among them is her passivity. Women may think they don't have to take initiative because the world will look after them.[1] When these wo-men think of "authorities," they are always "they," never "we." "Other voices and external truths prevail."[2] Belenky et al. describe the women who "search the eyes that watch them for reflections of themselves. They cannot get back behind their own eyes."[3] Because she finds her worth through others' response to her, such a woman commonly re-sponds "either by becoming like men or by becoming liked by men."[4] If she opts for trying to be liked, she will be rewarded for being nice and doing what's expected of her. The woman who "searches the eyes that watch her for reflections of herself" may suddenly see that she needs to work on *her* authority, not just respond to theirs. I remember vividly my own dawning awareness that I was so busy trying to do what other people thought was right that I was putting very little energy into what I myself thought ought to be done, and that the conflict between me and my efforts was draining my energy away. I hope that studies like this one, focusing on our experience of authority from within rather than observing the authority of others, will help women open their eyes.

Receiving women nurtured in the Christian tradition encounter a special problem in *the ideal of servanthood,* about which Susan Adams expressed strong feelings: "There are all these hackneyed things that don't ring true for me as a woman about 'servanthood' and about 'the authority of weakness' and 'servant among servants'... I'm rejecting those...as a woman." Under the soft blanket of "service," feelings of worthlessness often hide. Hungry for the caring and affirmation she isn't getting, the maternalistic woman fills her own void by taking care of others—whether they want it or not. Her "service" parodies the serving that freely responds to the perceived needs of others. Thus she has other tasks to perform before "servanthood" becomes an appropriate ideal. Note that the words "Whoever wants to be first must be last of all and servant of all" (Mk. 9:35) are spoken, not to women or children, but to the male disciples who are arguing with each other about who is the greatest. The Receiving woman needs to be able to say "no" before her "yes" is free. Only after a woman claims all that has been given her will she be able to "empty herself" appropriately. When a sense of abun-dance replaces her inner impoverishment, "service that is perfect free-dom" will become a possible and appropriate task for her.

As the Receiving woman begins to take a few baby steps toward Autonomy, she totters back and forth. She makes some solid efforts in her job or her family, but "deficit thinking" prevents her from appreciating her work.[5] She assumes that "What is important is what I have *not* done." If she is raising a family, for instance, the working world seems like the "real" place to be. As she takes a few more steps forward, she begins to want to validate her own efforts, but the only yardsticks she knows are those derived from male standards. She wants to be independent, but she feels driven to ask someone in authority to keep reassuring her that her independence is good.[6] She may want to beat the system, but she frames her wish without questioning the system's own terms. If a woman in this tottering stage has to make a choice between being self-effacing and allowing people to think she is pushy, she gives in and chooses the former.

Even some of the most powerful female leaders I interviewed told me stories about their difficult struggles to become confident. Dorothy McMahon recounted how deeply offended she was by a visitor to Australia who called God "She." She came to see that the offense she took sprang from a deep conviction that "God could not be anything like me." The struggles with confidence were by no means all ancient history. When under attack, confessed Dee Crabtree, "I just dispense with my authority." These stories encourage me to see myself as one of a great cloud of witnesses, strong and struggling women who take steps forward but sometimes stagger backward under the stresses they encounter.

When a Woman Moves into Autonomy

While their brothers were pressed toward a generally Autonomous posture quite early, women finally explode into it after they've concluded that they've had a bellyfull of passivity. Nobody ripped these women away from the comforts of early closeness. They heard few challenges to a heteronomous posture. Their experiences and their own inner processing finally led them to protest "It's about time!" and to push forward on their own with great energy. For many women, breaking through to Autonomous authority is their first conscious experience of authority. The awakening woman's anger not only energizes her but also provides her with a separate place from which to claim her own unique reality.

We can find these themes of energy, anger, encounter, and conflict in the stories of change women interviewees tell with excitement and enthusiasm.

Let's look more closely at what's happening to a woman as she bursts into Autonomous authority.

First, she turns away from a preoccupation with other people's authority, and even from other people's validation of her authority. She claims her own authority from the *inside*. Men have usually defined authority in external and institutional terms which are a poor fit for women who have moved decisively beyond the Receiving posture. The objective truths taught in our educational institutions carry the message "Submit." An appreciation for subjective truth invites us to listen to our own hearts and our own experience.

Now a woman begins to experience authority as *exousia*. The heteronomy and hiding that she has come to acknowledge as problematic for her were the *opposite* of "living out of one's essence." Her projections on male authority figures and male-dominated institutions had been a way of reserving a space for an important part of her life that she did not yet know how to claim. Now she reels in her line which she had cast out into institutions defined by men (the church, for example), pulls her authority out, unhooks it from the line, and holds it in her own hands.

Participants in a "Women as Leaders" education event who saw themselves as "moving toward Autonomy" said their images of God included themes of freedom and anger. For one it was important that "God has set us free." This clergywoman found herself "free to be an associate, in the midst of encouragement to try for [the post of] senior [minister] or free to go for senior, even if I fail." Another's image was that "God was very much present in my anger." For a third, "Jesus reclaiming the temple from the moneychangers" had become a luminous story.

Many women employ the metaphor, "I found my own voice," a voice long drowned out by others' voices. Because the newly Autonomous woman sees power as *having more to give,* once she has begun to hear her own inner voice, she wants to "hear others into speech," in Nelle Morton's words. Having themselves suffered from the assumption that "others know best," women who are growing into Autonomy want to avoid inflicting this assumption on their friends. (It is partly for this reason that a woman, having confided a difficulty to a man, often strongly resists a response that begins "Why don't you..." or "First, I would...")

But the Autonomous woman still has a way to go. Her enchantment with the discovery of her own way has yet to be dampened by the discovery that her inner voice is not infallible. After she has pressed the limits of this new internal pole of the tension, just as she did with the old external pole, she may arrive at a more complex and tensive resolution. She has set off on her own, like the fairytale princes who leave home to seek their fortune. Like all pilgrims she will discover that her destination looks very much like the starting place —to which her travels out and back will have given a radiant new dimension.

As a woman overcomes her inner resistance and begins to claim her authority, she begins to meet resistance from without. Dorothy McMahon has been asked "why I should have any sense of leadership or authority at all because God doesn't believe in women who are ordained anyway." Looking back, Dee Crabtree also remembers: "My authority was challenged every single time I opened my mouth."

Competent women begin to get the message that some men find them a threat. Ruth Shinn recalls an encounter in a groupwork class at Yale:

> I went to one of the professors and said such-and-such-a-thing had happened in a group and I was uncomfortable about it, and he looked at me and he said, "You've just got to come to terms with the fact that you're going to threaten any man you ever work with." Well, I was devastated when he said that—like, if I'm competent, that's going to make everybody else incompetent. I had the image of touching the sensitive plant and seeing it shrivel... It's a terrible thing to say about men that they can't function unless you put up a whole lot of flimflam to make them feel that they must excel on every single thing they ever do...

Verna Dozier also spoke of "threat" when I asked her: "Do you think you handle your authority in any ways that are distinctly yours because you are a *woman*?" After a moment to ponder she replied: I have a strange combination of being very warm and very threatening." I find her words a profound statement about female reality and male resistance to it. Why the resistance? To claim his male identity, a man must distance himself from his early dependence on female care. If this *warm* woman is the fount of good things, and if he must separate from that to claim his masculinity, the very attractiveness of her gifts becomes threatening. His need to separate himself from her drives him to belittle the good things she has to offer.[7]

We daily encounter (or at least dimly apprehend) the contradictions produced by that threat. Men call a woman domineering—but do not follow her. A woman's direct authority "often has a paradoxical effect on other adults: it is both emotionally powerful and ineffectual..."[8] Because woman's forcefulness is "irrationally overwhelming," "men...are prone to resist female authority and oppose its emotional force. Forceful directions from women in adult relationships are often labeled by men in ways that inhibit a woman's self-esteem: as bitchy, castrating, and the like."[9] A woman thus finds herself in a Catch-22 situation: she gets the message that others would prefer her to communicate with emotional distance, her self-esteem is shaken by men's negative response, the resultant anxiety increases her emotional expressiveness, and the negative response to her emotion gives her the message that it is "bad." Notice the consequences of these ancient and pervasive conflicts in everyday speech patterns. Both men and women devalue "women's talk." A woman's style tends to be hesitant, qualified, full of upward inflections and pauses that invite the other's response. The personal, prosaic, and practical content of her speech is evaluated as "trivial" when compared to more abstract and impersonal pronouncements. Men talk more—and interrupt more—while women listen and question, though our assumptions lead us to hear something quite different.[10]

Looking back over the interviews in the light of these powerful but often hidden dynamics, I'm not surprised that conflict over women's leadership is a major theme in three interviews, and the *only* common conflict theme I can discern.

Older women arrive at Autonomy with a new clarity, supported by the fact that they no longer occupy their old role in the society of the dominants. Aging women are no longer sex objects, and their wrinkles and gray hair do not earn the respect accorded their seasoned elder brothers. If they affirm their own value, they must do so as fully Autonomous people, having become even invisible to the eyes around them. I hear some mature and aging women saying that they have come to experience themselves as erotic creatures in a very Autonomous way, in contrast to their earlier sense that their sexuality emerged out of their relationship to *men*. As enfleshed and whole people, these fully ripened females now find the stage is paradoxically set for a full Autonomy that may previously have been obscured by admiring glances and their own appreciation of them.

Becoming Assertive

As a woman begins to hear her own inner voice, she pauses to attend to it before she speaks. Because I am "finding a new way," says Susan Adams, "I want to hold [these new ideas] in my head quite a lot before I put them out there..." But the time will come when she is ready to move past inner pondering, to speak out with the voice she has now claimed in her heart. To continue to sit on the sidelines and critique the way men exercise authority would be to persist in focusing on the authority of *others*. She knows she needs to press past abstract idealism toward addressing the actual dilemmas of authority that emerge in daily life. She makes a decision to act; to touch back to Joyce Yarrow's words, she "takes strength in her own self and makes it happen."

At this point, some of us go off the rails. Dorothy McMahon confessed that she had to explore the world of "power-tripping" before she could reject it. I got stuck in control, too. After vowing I would never succumb to what I had long identified as the male workaholic norms of the church world around me, I did just that. I found myself, as it were, holding on with white knuckles to a trapeze bar labeled "Do it right, do it now, do it all"—terrified that if I opened my clenched fists I would fall to disaster. Finally, I couldn't sleep because I was so anxious about accomplishing all the tasks in my overloaded life. I knew I had to get help. That decision held great power: I let go, and fell, not into disaster, but into a loving mystery that has surrounded me ever since. Now I can again allow myself to receive—help, and love, and the pleasures of work and of a whole life beyond work.

The "Women as Leaders" participants who identified themselves as "moving toward Assertion" had images of a God who upheld them as they took new risks. Said one, "God helps the weak to stand against the powerful...so She is on my side." For another, "God...doesn't interfere with my choices, but lets me grow and go forward on my own..." God is "encourager, cheerleader, coach," added another clergywoman. "God is a part of me." Still another was now drawn toward "God as Mother, whose embrace supports me in all endeavors" more than toward "the 'out there' Father I strive to please."

A woman who is moving toward Integration gets clearer about how she wants to exercise Assertive authority. Her position as an outsider arriving on the scene of society's power arrangements gives her a fresh vantage point that can assist her in the process of clarification. The people she works with may also enter into the fresh perspective she brings. Dorothy McMahon observed a lightening of expectations: "In some ways I have found it an advantage to be a woman because parishion-ers expect women clergy to do strange things. They think they know what clergymen will do in parishes but if a woman comes in they think, 'Oh well, I suppose she's a woman, she would try something a bit different,' and they will run with you."

A woman moving into a more active kind of authority in this open way begins to make some important distinctions. She distinguishes Assertion from aggression, ascertaining that behaving in a direct and competent manner is different from behaving aggressively.[11] She may also conclude that *control* is not what she's looking for. Control is power as an end in itself; but if she wants power in order to have more to give, power becomes a means, not an end. As she begins to see that it expands like love when it is shared, she gives power a new definition.

Her wish to critique Assertive authority as it is presented by the dominant culture will call forth all the independence and courage she can muster. The temptation to go along with what everybody knows is strong. It's easy to buy in on a power system that excludes you because the oppressed always wants what the oppressor has. Envy and the experience of powerlessness produce resentment that spirals downward. When I'm resentful, I am bound ever more deeply in oppression because I join the powers that be in defining myself as powerless. I need the courage to broaden my perspective beyond the boundaries of the game I'm losing.

As a woman brackets the rules of the old game and begins to imagine a new one, she may entertain some surprising ideas. For instance, she may question the idea that the best paid job, the job with the most prestige, is the one she ought to want.

Her new vision of assertiveness is different in several ways. First she *moves beyond the win-lose game*. She no longer covets the right to be one of the winners instead of one of the losers; now she envisions a whole new set of rules.

Second, *she stops ranking things hierarchically*. No longer assuming that if two things are different, one has to be better than the other, she now sees leadership as *another*, not a *higher* function. For many modern managers, the old assumption that "if we're not up, we're down" is shifting under the pressure of increasingly rapid change.[12] Now leaders increasingly see a need to invite and use the ideas and talents of people at every level of the organization. (Ironically, now that such new management approaches, originally associated with women's ways of leading, are more generally appreciated, they are increasingly divorced from their genesis in feminine attitudes.)

Discarding a view of leaders as separate and superior leads naturally to a third characteristic: *maintaining connectedness with the people*. Dorothy McMahon places a strong emphasis on "the authority of deeply connecting with the authentic feelings of people..." Women interviewees are profoundly conscious of their solidarity with their group and many, like Susan Adams, insist that their authority is given to them by the people.

This solidarity leads, fourth, to a vision of *leading from the center*. When I asked interviewees, "Do you see yourself as set over, apart from, or alongside the people you're working with?", two women suggested yet another possibility. Susan Adams saw the leader as "put within the middle...the authority is given to you from the edges...and you're accountable to them for it and how you use it." Verna Dozier saw herself as "set in the midst of" the people. "And that might be a feminine image," she continued, "because I see myself as a storyteller, as a hen gathering her chicks."

In summary, a woman's journey toward Assertive authority is slower than a man's, but she's less likely to get stuck at this stage. The Integrated intention to share authority is probably already part of her vision of Assertive authority. Now that she has found a way to "go for it," her journey moves with more power than we could ever have anticipated as we observed its beginnings.

A Man's Journey Toward Integrated Authority

In contrast to our conclusions about women, we may find, after we examine male patterns of growth through Assertive authority, that the journey was not as easy as we might have anticipated.

While women spoke at energetic length about the effects of femaleness or maleness on authority, men said little. After a little silence following my question, Jim Adams replied, "It's hard to imagine what life would be like as a woman." I frequently hear men downplaying differences between men and women, perhaps because they assume women are like them or because differences suggest troublesome questions or threaten these men's values for equality. Possibly, too, many men felt little engagement in the question about how gender is connected with authority because they saw it as somebody else's gut issue. (I recently heard a mature, sensitive man disclaim any significant personal interest in such a question: "I'm just trying to stay out of trouble.") Or perhaps, in contrast to women who found their concerns about authority impelling them outward toward action in their world, the men were moving inward to ponder these realities rather than making pronouncements about them.

When a Man Receives Authority

While many women in this stage find themselves responding to authority wielded by others, a number of men are exercising authority out of ready-made roles. Such a man benefits from permission to exercise authority and function as a leader, but he may experience some costs as well. In order to arrive at Integrated authority, he must learn to acknowledge God's authority and the authority of other people. If, however, a young man is taught that being on the receiving end is "womanish," if it threatens to pull him back into ancient dependence, he may quite naturally determine to resist it unequivocally—a determination that may later prove a mixed blessing at best. For the moment, however, both men exercising authority through Received roles and women who are subject to the authority of others may settle into a relatively comfortable accommodation. But each has a long way to go.

The Autonomous Male

Very early, most boys are pressed toward an Autonomous life posture—
even shamed into it, as they may have been shamed into giving up a
well-worn teddy bear. This early forcing puts the boy in a vulnerable
position; his Autonomy is often accompanied by a wound. Because he
was not allowed to move naturally through his need for dependence, for
an opportunity to receive, he needs others to hold the disallowed and
unresolved connected/receptive pole of the tension on his behalf. This
Autonomy, prematurely forced, sometimes feels more like a burden to a
man than like the "It's-about-time!" discovery it presents to a woman.

David McClelland describes the dynamics of the macho male in the
following way. Mother is the source of good things, and so the boy
"wants to be like whoever it is who has all the power to give him what he
wants." But society abruptly proscribes any such hankerings. Many
societies have provided almost surgical rituals in which the boy's "attachment to his mother and his identification with her" are "symbolically
broken by a severe initiation ceremony to make sure he assumes a male
identity."[13] Without such a ritual amputation, "exaggerated masculinity
of the macho type may occur as a form of defense against underlying
feminine traits" —a reaction that has been called "protest masculinity."[14]
And of course if such a man defines himself primarily as "not like her!"
we may conclude that his Autonomy is flawed and partial.

Picture a male leader with strengths that are commonly considered
"feminine" in our society (perhaps an INFP on the Myers-Briggs type
indicator)—an idealistic "defender of the faith" sort of person, adaptable
and compliant until someone threatens to violate his value system. Let's
picture this leader as a man in his 60s for whom cultural messages about
gender roles have been consistent over decades. Though our leader pos-
sesses inherent gifts of the "kinder, gentler" variety, he may be unable to
appreciate them, continually finding himself driven to prove "I am not a
wimp!" by threatening to "kick some ass around here." He may be all
the more dismayed because his wobble between those two sets of values
is held up to ridicule.

Many male pronouncements on leadership hold up autonomy as *the*
goal and fusion as *the* problem. While Autonomy as the antidote to
fusion may be exactly the right prescription for difficulties at one stage in
the journey, it is not a panacea. Recently I listened to some Canadian

clergymen questioning the usefulness of their acknowledged tendency to take distance. Unlike the women in that group, who confessed that when relationships went wrong, they tended to "take it personally," several men acknowledged that their response to interpersonal discomfort was to distance themselves, and that response left them feeling less pleased than perplexed. Perhaps clergymen, in a feminized institution and in a motherly role, may feel particularly desirous of distance and also discomfited by it.

While men seem strongly motivated to become autonomous, they also seem less wholehearted than their sisters in that enterprise. In contrast to a newly autonomous woman's desire to find freedom *for* taking charge of her life, a man often seems most concerned with freedom *from* others' efforts to take control of him.[15] His energy level seems lower than hers. A woman claims autonomy as good news; does a man accept it as an assigned burden?

Men seem lonelier than women as they move out in Autonomy. While women join with their sisters in seeking freedom-for, men, in their search for freedom-from, feel they must go it alone. I hear a great many clergymen accepting their lonely fate as leaders who must maintain professional distance from their congregations, and many clergywomen eager to emphasize that "pastor and parishioners are in this together." As I see it, the clergy role would seem to afford both community and self-differentiation, but the writings of Edwin Friedman, Bruce Reed, and John C. Harris convey a profound conviction that a clergyman is called to loneliness. David McClelland joins others[16] in pointing out how conflicted a man often feels about requesting and receiving guidance from a mentor, for instance. He wants the advice; he also wants to break with the mentor as soon as possible.[17] I have to conclude that these writers are describing a male, not a human, phenomenon. And I am led to wonder: is a man lonely partly because he is separated from the companion given to be with him (Gen. 2:18), and also, within his heart, from the connected pole of life for which she stands?

The Assertive Male

Men who live with Assertive authority discover that they are caught in the contradiction between promises and problems on several levels.

Interviewees acknowledged that it was an advantage to be male. Peter Sherer observed: "As a white middle-class male American, this brings with it enormous advantages in any political undertaking. The world in my experience is managed by those people. I always admire people outside the dominant group who take authority, and there are plenty of them...[but] if somebody said to me, 'You can trade in your demographics,' I would say, 'On the whole, no.'"

But maleness is perceived not only as an advantage but as a pressure that may oppress. Colin Bradford saw "masculinity" as a societal stereotype that contradicted his passionately held convictions about himself:

> People expect more aggressive, determined, imposing behavior from me than I am generally willing to give. I think of myself as a sensitive, nurturing, caring type of person and I have trouble being harsh...and demanding... But I generally avoid circumstances in which that's the kind of behavior that pays off. I'd much rather get behind somebody and help them, facilitate them, than...get above them and command them upward.

How natural not to want to trade in your male advantages and also not to want to suffer the disadvantages of being crammed into a "male" mold that doesn't fit!

Men are pressed toward exercising authority in the world around them; at the same time they hunger to touch the world inside them. While women moving into Autonomy may take time to savor and explore this newfound life posture, men find themselves pressed to get on with the action. (As in so many contexts where men tend to focus on external action while women attend to internal realities, here we clearly see one of the ways our body-selves express themselves—ways congruent with our physical reality but also extending way beyond it.) As we mature, the contrapuntal pattern of our growth leads us toward whole ness by embracing the strengths most fully developed by the other sex. We've noticed that women seek wholeness by expanding their repertoire beyond the nurturing of inner and spiritual realities to include acting in the world around them. A man's path leads him over the mountain, beyond the hard climb of Assertive action. If his Assertive way has led him to a controlling posture, he will yearn to be reconnected not only with the people he's been busy controlling, but with his own inner depths.

The alienation to be overcome is found not only within men, but between men and women. Men, who are pressed to assert themselves and take responsibility, discover that they are in conflict with women, not only because some women press for responsibilities denied them, but also because others abandon the Assertive territory to men and then sit on the sidelines and take potshots, or sulk, or condescendingly claim the moral high ground. Having accepted the risky task of moving into the public arena and attempting to meet its challenges, men take an understandably dim view of such women.

Men who live with Assertive authority may find themselves poised between still another set of promises and problems. Their zeal to succeed often carries beneath it a fear of failing. Thinking back over heady courtroom moments, Keith Mason reflected: "Certainly in a professional capacity you can be in full flight in a particular case and you can sort of stand outside yourself and say, 'Isn't he wonderful?' Usually that's just the second before you crash."

Remember Icarus? He took off toward the heavens powered by homemade wings made of bird feathers pasted together with wax. When he flew too near the sun's heat, the wax began to melt, and the feathers scattered. Icarus plummeted earthward. David McClelland sees the Icarus story as a prototype of the pattern Mason described: the heady "Isn't he wonderful?" moment, then the crash. The Icarus pattern expresses a man's buried neediness and vulnerability which, darkened and demonized by having been pushed out of sight, lurks as a pitfall in his path. But "Blessed are the poor in spirit." The threat holds not only disaster but also an invitation to wholeness, for behind what we desperately avoid a blessing often awaits.

A Man in the Transition between Assertive and Integrated Authority

The struggle with the promises and problems of Assertive authority may impel a man to reach out for an authority in which he can move first inward toward the promise of wholeness and then outward in a more open-handed way. David McClelland charts the path: "male competitiveness...should develop into losing one's self for a higher cause..."[18]

American citizens seemed to demonstrate a yearning for such a development in the presidential candidates they examined in the last election. Did these rivals really care about anything more than than they cared about winning? What did they want to win *for*? This crucial shift in goals also grasps the attention of the male interviewees who passionately recount their evolution past a preoccupation with getting their own way.

The man who is finding his way beyond competitiveness travels a path different from that pursued by most women. First he was driven to distinguish himself; now he seeks connection again. He has long claimed his own voice; now he seeks an authority in which others' voices find a place. In his earlier years he may not have known what it meant to adopt a receptive posture toward the authority of others (if he himself *was* one of the others); but now he might sometimes feel free to submit to the wisdom of other people.

As he begins to loosen his grip on power and reach out toward values he now sees as more compelling than power, he encounters difficulties and discomforts. It isn't easy to let go the need to appear always on top of things, always knowledgeable. Events often feel out of control because reality now appears less linear and rational. The control he knew and managed must now open up and make room for more players with different points of view.

In this transition, he has lost whatever comfortable sense of fit he enjoyed in the old symbiotic accommodation between dominants and subordinants, a fit that at least *felt* more to his advantage than these new unsettled conditions. The women he meets are now dotted all along the continuum between subordination and partnership.[19] How is he to find out what these awakened women want? This new task feels difficult and discomfiting. He is newly reluctant to engage with subordinant women who threaten to drag him back into that destructive place from which he has barely extricated himself. Not only women, but men, too, are scattered all over the map. The old comfortable male consensus has dissolved. Fully developed males receive few rousing cheers; instead they may find themselves judged impotent by conventional standards. The energy balance has shifted: no longer do dominant men receive respect from subordinant women; now we see newly energized women regarded with puzzled doubt by men who don't feel very good about what's happening—men who may be feeling bewilderment, pain, stress, fear, and anger.

In summary, as I look back on the journey of women and men from Received through Autonomous and Assertive authority, I am struck by the difficulty with which women claim Assertive authority and the difficulty with which men let it go.

Women and Men in Integrated Authority

As we grow into Integrated authority, our experiences are more similar than distinct. But, since our discovery of Integrated authority is shaped by the journey that led us toward this point, it will be illuminating to describe women's experience and men's experience of Integrated authority in the light of their stories thus far.

Five Characteristics of Women with Integrated Authority

1. *These women want more power so that they will have more to give.*

As David McClelland points out, many women have wanted to share their resources all along. Now they want power so they can have *more* resources to share. In contrast, he holds, "The notion of scarcity of resources and of external material supplies that are exhausted in giving seems more likely to be a male concept,"[20] and he cites the experience of nursing mothers—suckling their babies produces more milk. Note, by contrast, that men's sexual experience ends in being exhausted or spent. In this and many other ways, our broader life experiences are intimately incarnate in our bodily and especially our sexual experiences.

   Not only do women tend to want more so they can give more, they find that by empowering others they empower themselves; this discovery moves them away from an either/or posture ("If I have power it means you can't") toward a both/and *"We* have power." As Dee Crabtree surmised, "Using authority in a way which is integrated with the community and not over against, I suspect, may be related to being a woman." Insofar, therefore, as women receive their Assertive authority *as a means of mutual empowerment,* their Assertiveness easily moves them into Integrated authority.

2. *Arriving at Integrated authority means resolving some of the tension between self and others.*

Many of these women have pursued a zig-zag course like a sailboat's. A woman typically tacks from

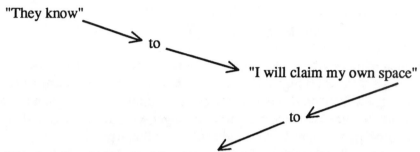

"They know"

to

"I will claim my own space"

to

"Truth comes from *a dialogue between my wisdom and that of others*"

...a position in which, as one woman put it, "You let the inside out and the outside in."[21] She has arrived at a new place in which she can integrate what she has found inside herself with what she has learned from outside sources.

This Integrated way of knowing moves women into an interdependent relationship with others. Mothers start acting like *friends*. They learn that they can become stronger through empowering their children, and, as they discover that they have resources, they look for them in their offspring. Mothers who had arrived at this stage now had a different *way* of being helpful: they tried to help their daughters "on the daughters' own terms" and evoked their children's growth through asking them questions.[22] Question-posing, often regarded as the behavior of powerless people, is in fact a powerful way of eliciting the growth of another. (I think here of Jesus' evocative questions, or Socrates' method, or adult educators' care in framing the right question for group discussion, or even of the many interviewees who told me the interview process itself had been an important medium of growth for them.) In contrast, mothers who had little sense of their own authority found their children's questions *stressful*.

It's as though these women arriving at Integrated authority are discovering that *there really is a lot of room in God's world*. As they look back, Integrated people often conclude that "We drew the circle

smaller than we had to and became competitive when it was not necessary." Now they find that claiming one's own authority while providing
hospitable space in which the authority of others can blossom provides a
paradoxical and gratifying resolution of the self-other contradictions that
earlier seemed paralyzing.

3. *Integration means living with paradox.*

Women at this stage of development, say the authors of *Women's Ways
of Knowing,* "show a high tolerance for internal contradiction and ambiguity. They abandon completely the either/or thinking so common to the
previous positions described... They no longer want to suppress or deny
aspects of the self in order to avoid conflict or simplify their lives..."[23]
    Several characteristics of a woman's life combine to help her
become comfortable with paradox. Like members of any nonelite group,
she grew up with two pictures of "how things are": the dominant male
culture's picture and her own picture. Finally she has found that she
cannot accept without question the picture that was handed to her: in
many important ways, that picture contradicts her own experience, and
she is compelled to make sense of the discrepancies. While her brothers
may be presented with one clear picture, the woman's wrestling with her
dual socialization—as a resident in the dominant world and as an inhabit-
ant of her own world—prepares her to *expect* many understandings of
life to be ambiguous and even contradictory.
    A woman's tendency toward nondualistic assumptions also in-
creases her level of comfort with complex pictures and dissuades her
from settling into a triumphal Assertive life posture. A woman tends to
hold disparate realities together with some comfort, in contrast to the
male tendency toward either/or postures; she will live with this-AND-
that, even when it isn't clear how they fit together, while her brother may
be more prone to decide "I'm *not* going to do *this* any longer. From now
on I'll do THAT." The ease with which he can discriminate the arenas
of his life, select a clear focus, and "major" in it contrasts with the
multiplicity of her daily life. Many mature women "are struggling to
conduct both creative and relational activities in a busy schedule divided
between family life and highly individualized work... The ability to
tolerate ambiguity, to transcend paradox and to engage conflict with

humor are the special characteristics of greater reflective understanding at these stages."[24]

Placing a high value on process as well as product also increases a woman's tolerance for ambiguity and paradox. Enterprises can seem simple when construed under the heading of "goals"; but the *way* things move along into the future gathers up all the complexities of our inner and interpersonal experiences as they are played out within events. Rather than getting on top of the situation with a theory and mentally deleting all the bits that won't fit, a woman more easily consents to move trustfully through a process in which the present looks murky and the outcome is yet to unfold. Of course, there are men who experience a gap between their reality and the official picture, resist either/or approaches, and stay close to the murkiness and multiplicity of life on-the-way; but women's lives make these postures more difficult to avoid.

"Women as Leaders" participants who saw themselves as moving toward Integration presented paradoxical images of God and of the gifts they had received. They described God and themselves as "feminine and powerful," having "power without control." "God's will is that all are free to think and choose," said one. Another now knew deeply that "being too controlling/playing God is inappropriate." One described a call to be "strong and appropriately vulnerable." "Trust in God's absolute LOVE helps free me to heal wounds, take risks, be vulnerable." Another woman found an appropriate symbol in God as eagle "who cares, who challenges, teaching me to fly."

Seeing that the situation is paradoxical, the Integrated woman feels pressed to discover some strategies for living with the contradictions, developing a wide range of possible responses, and selecting the one that seems to show most promise for the immediate situation. She has developed enough flexibility and enough options to respond to *what is*. She may sometimes choose to respond in a way expected of subordinates—especially under circumstances like these: when her boss won't listen, when there isn't time to work through to a more satisfying relationship (or she judges that it would take more energy than she chooses to invest), when she decides that the cost of confrontation is too high or when she is just worn down by the endlessness of the struggle.

Her strategies include not only analyzing and responding to the external situation but understanding her own feelings, learning how they affect others, and growing in the ability to make choices about how she will express them. When a woman finally "comes to herself," has claimed her own reality and is ready to proclaim it, she may burst forth in anger and pain in such an emotionally loaded way that the man to whom she is speaking finds himself more preoccupied with how to fend off, decipher, or simply bear the bundle of emotions than with hearing the content of her communication. As she reflects on her distress in such encounters, such a woman will discover she can make choices about how she wants to communicate. She may decide to learn how to deliver her messages with sufficient self-possession to increase her chances of being heard. She may learn to express her emotions along the way so that she does not arrive at crucial encounters feeling so loaded up. Or she might conclude that her emotionality is appropriate and set about challenging the norm that people ought to convey their messages dispassionately. Discovering that she has many options, the Integrated woman will make her choices and develop her strategy.

A recent letter from a friend in Australia nudged me to become clearer about strategies I want to adopt. My friend, who works in a denominational agency, wrote that she had been seeking other women's reflections on how she might persist in her efforts to work collaboratively when those efforts had to be pursued within a political environment that she perceived as "largely about power and control and influence." "I know that is a sweeping statement," she continued, "that there are many exceptions and that my experience is limited. But my dilemma is, when I try to work collaboratively and I am patronized or have the credit for my work taken from me, then do I retreat, fight back, try to beat them at their own game or what?"

Perhaps it was because those words came from 12,000 miles away that they jolted me into some objectivity. I found myself admitting that I am tempted to make all the responses she described, and I can think of times when I do all those things. But then came the thought, "*This* is what I *need* to do: 1. Name what is happening; 2. Strive to keep on living according to my values in spite of the pressures to do otherwise; 3. Seek enough support so that I can do the first two things." As I keep practicing "naming it," I find I am increasingly able to do so gently but clearly when that seems most useful, planning how to make myself heard rather than allowing my "naming" to burst out in a way that intimidates or produces unmanageable anxiety in the other. I can object to the other's behavior without framing him as the enemy. (If the requirement for all this careful strategy seems unfair to women, we might remind ourselves that subordinates have to serve as teachers of dominants— whether it's fair or not.)

As a woman grows in her ability to live with the contradictions life brings and discern and practice appropriate strategies, she is increasingly able to bring to bear any one of a broad range of strengths.

4. *She can exercise Received, Autonomous, and Assertive authority for the sake of Integrated goals.*

Here is an everyday example of how all those ways of exercising authority fit together in the experience of a clergywoman. She said, "I preach out of my own experience...thus I say to the people in the congregation, 'This is what I expect from you; not conformity to my ideas but honest reflection upon your own experience.'" (Note the evocative stance from a position alongside the parishioners.) "When I first came, the complaints about my sermons were that they were too emotional and personal. But...I continued to preach that way until the people in my congregation began to see that what I was doing was affirming their right to reflect seriously upon their own faith experiences."[25] This woman demonstrates Assertive authority grounded in her Autonomous conviction about what kind of preaching would be most useful to her parishioners. She exercises gentle Assertiveness to bring about Integrated evocative goals.

Let's look now at a biblical story that illustrates the exercise of Received, Autonomous, Assertive, and Integrated authority, with a hint of the complex movement toward Integration. The conversation between Martha and Jesus in John 11:17-27 shows both partners in the dialogue pressing beyond conventional assertions. As teacher Jesus works with Martha step by step in an evocative manner, while Martha hangs in, struggles, and responds. Martha begins with Received knowledge, reciting what she has been taught: "I know that he will rise again in the resurrection on the last day." In an "I am" statement, Jesus moves that pious generality to an affirmation pointed right at Martha's present distress: "I am the resurrection and the life." He defines himself in relation to Martha's grief for her brother. His affirmation assists Martha to shift from Received knowledge ("They say") to Autonomous knowledge ("I know"). Notice how Jesus works with her subtly, gently, evocatively. For Martha, Received and Autonomous knowledge come together in a powerful insight: "Yes, Lord, I believe." As mind and heart converge, Martha suddenly becomes a "passionate knower,"[26] one who enters into union with the known.

This story illustrates the intricate movement from conventional to subjective knowledge and on to the joining of these two ways of knowing in paradoxical resolution. The story is about knowing; it is also a story about a loving and transforming friendship in which knowledge and relationship become one, and love and truth are joined in an ecstatic moment.

5. *A woman in the stage of Integrated authority has a sense of abundance and of her own goodness.*

She takes pleasure in her many-faceted responsibilities—strongly motivated work, intimate relationships, and the tasks of maintaining her home. She also takes pleasure in her ability to enter those arenas ready to respond and act in whatever way promises to be most useful right now: to receive and connect with others, to define herself and "stay on her own thread," or to speak out boldly and work toward her chosen ends. In the fruitfulness and flexibility of her way of living she arrives at a "belief in her own goodness" that expands her open interest in the development of others.[27]

This new interest in caring for others differs radically from the service that had earlier been motivated by her inner poverty. Several women have resonated with this homely experience: I remember a time when I would unquestioningly make the coffee in the office, then a time when I would *not* make the coffee. Now I might or might not, but it's not a big deal and I have a choice. The Integrated woman's care for us out of her abundance is free of the entrapment and distortion we experience from people whose internal transactions spring from a need to compensate for their own impoverishment—whether they be maternalistic women with low self-esteem or men ripped away too early, forced to tough it out.

Because she is not hanging on to authority roles as a way of justifying herself, she can now hold them lightly. Authority is given for a purpose, and she can open her hands and let the authority role go when it has done its work on behalf of others' development. The authority of a mother, for example, is a temporary authority. She is working herself out of a job—working toward equality with her child. In that process, she will find herself teaching the child both to respect and to challenge authority—including her own! What a different way of holding authority than desperately hanging on to a role for the status it affords!

The joy she feels in exercising authority *as a woman* shines forth in Dorothy McMahon's story about how she came to believe in her own goodness:

> My whole experience of the women's movement in the late sixties and onwards was a major transformation in terms of my own self-awareness, my own confidence as a human being. I connected with some of my own pain and my own inner worth. Probably one of the real turning points was very early on when a woman who was a feminist came out from England. She called God "She," and I was so offended! I felt that was a dreadful and blasphemous thing. Someone challenged me: what did my reaction say about my perception of myself? *Why* did I find it that shocking? And I faced the fact that it was because my own self-esteem was so low that I didn't want to associate a woman with God; I didn't want to associate myself with the nature of God. I tackled that over quite a period of time, and I came through to perceiving the link between female-ness and God, and therefore myself and God. God became imma-nent for me at that point... I could witness to my faith, because I was living out of it from within, and so that gave me a new sense of authority which did come from that experience of the God who was within and who was as female as male.

Note these qualities in Dorothy's story: she moves away from an assumption that "authority belongs to others"; she knows that authority is received from God; she is able to make the claim "*I* receive it"; and she confidently proclaims her convictions.

We see Integrated women like Dorothy McMahon owning their authority in a new way—a way that's different from those who don't take the risk of owning authority at all, different from those who content themselves with internal processing, different from those who get into the game and play by men's rules, different from those who adopt others' aggressive postures as their own, different from those who want to fight with men and show them up, and different from those who deny they stand in the need of support.

Five Characteristics of Men with Integrated Authority

I found many sources from which to draw a picture of women in Integrated Authority, but I don't know any secondary sources that describe what it means for *men* (as distinct from people in general) to arrive at mature exercise of authority. Thus I was driven back to the interviews to learn directly from these eight men what it means for them to have arrived at Integrated authority. Again, five primary characteristics emerged.

1. *An Integrated man resolves the confusion between Assertion and aggression.*

We don't commonly think of clergy as having aggressive occupations, but perceiving that there are aggressive possibilities in the role, our clergymen are determined to avoid them. Jim Adams has found that pushing to get his way doesn't accomplish what he hoped for; instead, he reported, "I just get into a fight..." When Adams supports people, on the other hand, lots gets done, though it might not be just what he had in mind. Admitting that "In my early days I might have wanted to dominate," Glenn Farquhar-Nicol discovered that was self-defeating: people responded to being "hit over the head" by questioning his authority. Though he has rejected his previous dominating posture, Glenn cares deeply about being Assertive, as his forthright description of his strengths demonstrates.

> The reason I'm called into disputes is not because of role but because people know I have integrity, they can trust I will see things reasonably, objectively, and fairly. People respect me for my wisdom. Loyalty is tied in: I've stuck with people and they know that...I've begun to recognize I have these gifts—God given...I'm a person of vision and I'm always thinking of where we ought to be heading...

Glenn seeks a model in the strongly assertive but consistently non-aggressive picture of Jesus he sees in the Gospels.

Laymen like Keith Mason provide a clear picture of the hard work involved in staying Assertive without pushing into aggressiveness or abandoning the responsibility to simply hang in amid the difficulties. In his efforts to get the Law Reform commissioners to turn in their reports on time, Mason describes the many ways he can get off target. Sometimes he has walked away from a conflict, looked back later, and realized "I shouldn't have." At other times, out of his frustration at his inability to get the commissioners to submit reports, he would "take over the job, in effect: 'If you're not going to do it, I'm going to go ahead and get it done.' And yet it was their baby, and I had no responsibility to do it." At other times he took his frustration to a third party, and realized that was off target too. "I never actually went up to them and said, 'Look, what you are doing is a disgrace,' although at times I would admit to others that I felt they could have done more. It really wasn't a terribly honest way of going about the problem." He confronts these issues, not only in the workplace, but in the diocese, where he must strive to be Assertive in the face of a hierarchy he perceives as unjust and aggressive.

Colin Bradford also contends with the aggressive power of institutions. Colin acknowledges: "...if you've got a profit and loss situation and the company is about to fold, you've got to fire people, there's no doubt about it. But...the normal crushing circumstances that managers face are much more arbitrary than that. They have to do mostly with fiefdoms and bureaucratic battles and stuff like that, and that's part of the real world, but I think larger people ought to be able to think beyond those..."

In spite of the dilemmas they encounter, many of these men prove through their actions that they have learned to discriminate Assertion from aggression. Some of their stories describe complex actions within institutions, as when Peter Sherer describes his efforts to "minimize the steamroller effect of the institution" on the person he has to fire. And some stories of Assertion are as simple as Dwight Lundgren's response when his father found he couldn't keep his commitment to preach on Laymen's Sunday: "I'll do it."

2. *Integrated authority means moving beyond hierarchical assumptions.*

Not only does he reject aggression (power *against*); he also rejects hierarchy, in which control and ranking combine to exert power *over*. The negative consequences of exercising hierarchical authority were dramatized for Jim Adams by a parishioner's challenge: "When you start quoting canons, bylaws, and contracts to me, we are having a fight. We are not working something out. When you start talking about your authority as the priest and the rector you are becoming oppressive, and you are going to get a negative and hostile reaction."

In contrast, says Adams, "The authority that I like and enjoy and that I think is effective is not hierarchy but connection authority. I don't feel I've got the kind of authority that an army general or the CEO of a corporation has. I wouldn't know what to do with it if I did..."

These men find that turning their backs on the accepted hierarchical system holds not only promise but cost. Adams acknowledges that he is relinquishing some of the rewards of proclaiming wisdom from on high. His quiet, collaborative way of exercising authority does not yield "a pleasant or exciting feeling like I have when I'm lecturing and people are looking at me eagerly with upturned faces... That kind of teaching is very affirming for me, but I don't think it does them a whole lot of good."

In academia Colin Bradford also experienced the costs of putting himself at odds with the hierarchical system and defying its control and ranking:

> I haven't conformed, and I don't do standard economics... So it's a very different view and it didn't fit well and it didn't go down well in the discipline... And as one of my best colleagues put it, Bradford...may be right, but he's in a no-man's land...[It's thought his work] doesn't *fit* conventional standards, ergo it doesn't *make it* by conventional standards...

Bucking the Control culture results in punishment: "It took me years to figure out why I was getting this kind of flak... Now I've gotten very used to it. What I've done is I've accepted that my work is original...and therefore it generates...almost always...from conventional academics... very strong criticism."

As he moved from a more authoritarian stance toward a new posture of "getting alongside people," seeing himself "as one member with a particular function," Glenn Farquhar-Nicol found his relinquishment of hierarchical authority did not endear him to some parishioners who demanded: "Tell us exactly what you want us to do." He refused. In the end, collaborative work with the parish council yielded support for Glenn's non-hierarchical position.

As he worked to maintain his nonhierarchical stance, Jim Adams' vestry pressed him to adopt a more complexified and sophisticated strategy:

> For a long time I tried to get people to say what they thought and held my own opinions to myself. Then the vestry accused me of withholding and treating them contemptuously. They said. 'You hold your opinions back because you think that we can't handle them...' Now, as soon as I have a position, I try to state it calmly as just my opinion. Then I try to detach myself emotionally from my position so that other people can sharpen what they think.

Adams' strategy provides a useful example of a leader who brings together Assertive and Receiving strengths in the service of Integrated, evocative goals.

3. *These men are supporting women, not from above, but from alongside.*

While supporting women did not emerge as a *primary* concern for these men, several comments do affirm its presence.

Howard Ashby told the story of how he shifted to a new set of cultural values as he moved from from the traditional patriarchal norms of his Maori village to the very different ideas about partnership espoused at St. John's Theological College:

> I had one of the toughest areas in New Zealand here, in the whole north, where there's no women allowed even to stand up and read in the church. Certain ones are appointed to dust around the altar or around the sanctuary. Nobody else was allowed to go and clean it.

So that was very difficult when I came here [to St. John's College] to accept that [*i.e., women in ministry*]. On the marae no women stand to talk... At St. John's here they...gave me a new eye-opener...I felt good to be able to work with women and to share in the services.

I often hear men, out of egalitarian motives, denying that there are any differences between men and women. Bradford holds it is "abso-lutely crazy...to genderize" these issues. "Why women should be seen as having to be sensitive, nurturing, caring, supportive always and every-where and at all times with all people,...that's just nuts."

Peter Sherer, recognizing his advantage as a white male, expresses admiration for those who lead without that advantage: "People...will cede their authority to me more easily than they would to an Hispanic woman, for instance. I always admire people outside the dominant group who take authority, and there are plenty of them." Jim Adams voices not only support for women but also identification with them: "It's hard to imagine what life would be like as a woman, but I think a lot of my authority is more feminine than masculine, if I read your...book [*Sexual Paradox*] correctly. The authority that I...enjoy and...think is effective is...connection authority... In many respects I think the kind of authority I have is more motherly than fatherly."

4. *Men in Integrated Authority rediscover their ability to Receive.*

As men become able to Receive again, they find opened up before them new spiritual depths that had not been accessible when their lives were all filled up with making things happen.

The Receiving posture takes a variety of forms among these men who exercise Integrated authority; some examples follow.

Peter Sherer was aware that *he didn't invent his gifts—he had re-ceived them from God.* Messages from his family and school had de-livered a clear message: "Figure out what your gifts are and use them."

Colin Bradford found himself impelled toward *a receptive way to learn.* As he sought to understand the causes of rapid economic growth in countries like Korea, Colin began by looking "at what was actually going on in the country" rather than by first positioning himself within the framework of previously established economic theory. "The more conventional view of originality in economics at least...in academic life is to read your way...thoroughly into the literature and then make a contribution within an already defined literature. That presumes that the literature is right." The conventional approach was illustrated by a colleague with whom Colin had recently lunched: "he just volunteered the fact that what he was doing was reading the literature and...trying to find a niche that was unfilled and then filling in the niche. And that's the way you make it in academic [life]." Bradford reported that his own approach "has cost me plenty." After his initial astonishment and dismay at the punitive sanctions, he has come to the point where he can say "I've gotten now so that I can handle it and expect it and when it happens I just can trust that there is an answer."

Bradford also *carried his Receiving posture into his role as a teacher concerned to evoke the wisdom of the student.* When students act as though professors were knowledgeable on almost everything, "one needs to throw it back on the person and say,...'What do you think?'"

A hospitable receptive posture was the primary characteristic of Dwight Lundgren's ministry. With Barnabas' encouraging style as a model, Lundgren saw himself as hanging around people, comfortable with where they were at the moment, until "the appropriate, providential time when they're ready to talk..." He saw institutional tasks as full of space where people's life agendas could be welcomed. Seeing himself as the servant of the community, he could reflect on an angry outburst, "She just needed someone to unload on," accepting the woman's anger without retreating into passivity.

Sherer knew his gifts were received; Bradford's knowledge began with a receptive posture toward "what is"; Lundgren received his parishioners' very being as pastor, leader, and community servant. In a way, Howard Ashby provides a summary for all those ways of receiving, for he *sees all his own works included in God's gifts.* Ashby found a metaphor in a Maori saying about the kumara (sweet potato): "They'll say a kumara will never speak of his own sweetness...we never talk about 'Now we've done this.' To me it's just part of God's work." People who know their lives are received from God don't show off. God is their point of reference, and this helps them avoid problematic sides of Receiving (seeking others' approval) and of Assertion (striving to impress other people).

Sometimes the rediscovered Receiving posture of Integrated men seems connected with women and the recovery of feminine gifts that had been pushed off to the side. While working with Church of England rectors and vicars who were reflecting on their new experience of working with female deacons, I heard the men say that they were now finding themselves pressed to be whole people on the job. Formerly, when collaborating with another clergyman on an occasional ecclesiastical enterprise, they got right to the task and, on dispatching it, retired to their solitary roles. Now, though at first they resisted dealing with their feelings and with their relationship with their new female colleague, the women deacons gently left them no option. I was moved by the men's expressions of positive feelings about their resulting sense of a newfound wholeness.

All those varied experiences of Receiving rediscovered seem ultimately rooted in a Receiving posture toward God, which each man described in his own way. As a strong thinker, Dwight Lundgren found himself "always wondering." "What do *we* know about God?" he asked, more than once. His Receiving posture took the form of *accepting the mystery,* with a certain awe-filled lightness ("I think of myself as kind of a court jester"; "We're all fools for Christ"). In Dwight's wondering, Receiving posture, there was no room for Messianism.

Glenn Farquhar-Nicol's Receiving took a form more congenial to an affective personality: *a daily half hour in silence within which relationships were healed and his balance was restored.* "I spend that time on angers and hurts so I don't have ongoing conflicts." He could reach down past any present trouble to the deep affirmation that lay below it.

For Jim Adams, Receiving meant *acknowledging his helplessness and emptiness, and knowing himself nevertheless supported:* "Sometimes I am able to withhold my attempts at controlling life and trying to be somebody." At such times he may know himself supported by God: "I associate God with the experience of being supported and substantiated from a source above, beyond, and under myself."

For these Integrated men, Receiving is not an *alternative* to Assertion but joined with it in a graceful resolution of the contradiction they experienced earlier. Let us examine some of the shapes this resolution takes in the men's experiences.

In Colin Bradford's "looking at the world and responding to it," Receiving, Autonomy, and Assertion are joined in a single cognitive act.

Simply looking at what is, interpreting the reality out of his Autonomous perceptions, and speaking out about his conclusions—all these elements flow together in an Integrated process that threatens the conventional procedures dominated by control and ranking.

Notice the paradoxical *mutuality* in Glenn Farquhar-Nicol's pastoral approach. When people try to sidestep their decisions by projecting their authority on him he eschews both passivity and control and "immediately throws it back in their court... It's a middle ground—not 'I'll decide for you' or 'You go away and decide.' I might suggest options they hadn't thought of. If they're not willing to look at those options, that's up to them."

Three interviewees describe the step backward to Receive and the step forward into action as movements in an easy dance. Listen to Peter Sherer reflect on the way he handles his initiative in a group discussion:

> I have a tendency to...say enough of what I think needs to be said to get the conversation rolling, but I feel that the answer will appear out of the group as long as I keep holding onto the fact that that's where we're going, toward some sort of answer...[Notice the evocative quality of his initiative and compare it to an opening statement from a leader bent on control.] When I'm in a group and not leading it,...I always empathize with the leadership. So if the leadership asks the question and there's this pause, I come to my thought immediately, wait a decent interval to see if there's somebody else who's got something to say, and usually they don't and so—bang! —I'm the first one, hopefully not only saying it in a way that says what I [want to] say but engages other people to join the conversation... And when I'm not the one taking the first step forward I'm very, very conscious of the one who *is* and very aware of taking my step forward in support of whoever took the first step.

Colin Bradford describes a similar dance as he tells of his political initiative in a small town on the Connecticut shore:

> The other place I guess I've really exercised authority is in politics in Guilford, Connecticut.... I went out and listened to what the hell was bothering people. And what was bothering them was they wanted good schools and they didn't want to pay for them. And I

started campaigning..., saying "Let's pay for them." And in a
Republican town...as a Democrat, with a Democratic message—
"Let's raise taxes and pay for our kids' schooling"—I got elected
twice... We got our budget through. And you know I really managed to mobilize the bloody town to do something they basically
didn't want to do. And you know there is a kind of—again—
authority... The authority comes by finding not only your own
voice internally, but it's gathering other people's voices into who
you are speaking for... That is a very powerful form of authority.
That enables a community to get going doing something which it
should do for itself which it wasn't willing to do...

For Jim Adams, the dance takes shape as he ponders the interplay
between his own goals, the initiatives of others, and the process of parish
life:

If you are faithful to attending the process, goals may occasionally
attach themselves to you. Goals appear. I rarely get attached to
them, and when I do, it just causes trouble... Actually I have a
goal—that by the time I retire, this place would have about twice as
many people as now. But it's no big deal. I don't lie awake nights
thinking about how to make that happen... If the congregation were
twice as big, it might be more substantial. But it might be just
another way of my trying to achieve immortality, leaving behind
something that is more impressive than when I came.

Notice the lightness with which he prepares to hold any goals that may
"appear," and his suspicion of any attachment to them. Observing the
interplay between his own "steps forward" and his wish to invite others'
initiatives has led Adams to a sophisticated picture of a nonhierarchical
style: "Now, as soon as I have a position, I try to state it calmly as just
my opinion. They I try to detach myself emotionally from my position
so that other people can sharpen what they think."
  Those who find themselves flipping back and forth between an
"enabling" and a "take charge" stance would do well to study that
statement. For the Integrated leader, those two postures are not simple
alternatives; careful attention to the interplay between initiative and
hospitable receptiveness yields leadership strategies that will transcend
control and passivity and serve Integrated purposes.

As these men join Receiving and Assertion, they discover power that is both simple and sophisticated. At earlier stages, many men thought they had to take hold and steer clear of a receptive "feminine" posture. When those apparent opposites are reunited, there emerges a graceful resolution to the basic masculine problem—a problem that echoes the problem within women and the problem between women and men. Not only men, but women, too (and perhaps especially), will benefit from looking long and hard at the sophisticated efforts of leaders like Adams. Because they have often been at it longer and have received and taken more opportunities to experiment with the exercise of power and authority, men who have achieved expertise in their inhabiting of Integrated authority can provide helpful examples for all of us.

5. *The men find a model in the picture of Jesus, who gives up power and holds all power.*

This fascinates me: men spoke of Jesus as their model, while women did not. (See, in contrast, the different and varied images of God described by the "Women as Leaders" participants.) Some women have been offended when I reported this observation, and it may indeed be a coincidence. This is a small sample. But I do remember that when participants in classes on authority described childhood authority figures, the women described women and the men told stories of men.

Let's set the stage for this picture of self-definition and self-emptying by recalling the story about Jesus in Mark 8:27-9:1. When Peter said, "You are the Messiah," Jesus "began to teach them that the Son of Man must undergo great suffering, and be rejected...and be killed... And Peter took him aside and began to rebuke him. But turning and looking at his disciples, he rebuked Peter and said, 'Get behind me, Satan!'" Jesus here redefines his role in contrast to the cultural expectation that the Messiah would burst forth on the scene as a victorious figure. Instead he vigorously puts forth the paradox enshrined in the familiar Palm Sunday hymn:

> Ride on! Ride on in majesty!
> In lowly pomp ride on to die.

When Integrated authority confronts the Control culture without the
Control culture's methods, the inevitable result is suffering. This story in
Mark's gospel, which I suggest as a paradigm of Integrated authority in a
man, is echoed by the interviewees, who find Jesus a model for their
lives. Jim Adams looks to Jesus as one who relinquished power:

> ...In the unfolding story we can see the way the disciples discovered
> their own authority in spite of themselves because Jesus refused to
> be the answer for them. That's the best model I know. That's the
> power of the gospels' story of Jesus, "who thought equality with
> God not a thing to be grasped, but emptied himself and became one
> of us."

But what stands out for Colin Bradford is the model of Christ as
"the consummate hero—somebody who was willing to go to the wall and
die for what he believed in... Because I think most of all... I'd really like
to be a hero. [But that's a costly choice.] And maybe I've sort of latched
onto this way of doing it, which is pretty scary, a pretty difficult way of
choosing to live your life."

In response to my question whether he could think of stories or
passages in the Bible that reminded him of what he'd been telling me
about his authority, Glenn Farquhar-Nicol draws the pictures of the self-
emptying One and the Hero together.

> The footwashing is an obvious one. The passion stories. I look at
> footwashing: being a leader is being a servant. But not hiding in
> the corner and doing the dishes and leaving a vacuum. When Jesus
> washed feet, people were in no doubt that this was the master... The
> last third of the gospels is about things being done to Jesus. Still he
> arrived in that position because of his activity, not because of his
> passivity. I think probably because of the Protestant focus on the
> cross, rather than on Jesus' activity leading to the cross, we have
> made too much of the powerless notion. There's a tension in the
> leadership of Jesus and myself. He is recognized as teacher, has
> authority, still he calls out of them their own power and energy.
> [He asks:] "What do you want?" That [question] doesn't just let
> him take over. The parables call for people to participate in the
> story. It's much more mutual teaching than in the authoritarian

models. It's direct leadership; yet servanthood is about calling forth
what is in others. It's radically different from leaving a vacuum:
someone will then exercise leadership.

Glenn's picture of "active powerlessness" stands in contrast to both authoritarianism and passive "enablement."

In a sort of "double twist," Peter Sherer presents a picture of Jesus
as one who evokes Peter's role as an evocative leader:

It seems looking back at the common thread of circumstances in
which I exercised my authority, the theme is bringing resources to
the politically unable. I'm sort of a big brother... I had an interest-
ing vision of my relationship to Jesus: Jesus to me now is a younger brother—wise, supportive, who reminds me that my role is to be
an older brother.

In this contrapuntal picture, Jesus models for Peter the kenosis Peter
feels called to. All these images of Jesus bring the Gospel story to bear
on the men's own discovery that they can be open, receptive, and evocative—and at the same time active, assertive, and heroic.

Women and Men Together in Integrated Authority

Out of the encounter between women socialized to Receive and men
socialized to Assert—an encounter that issues in painful contradictions,
anger and conflict, resentment and contempt—arises a tensive situation
in which change may be born—change within and between men and
women.

As mature men and women, both seeking to change and grow, join
their journeys and begin to walk side by side, everyone can be a winner.
Male Autonomy and Assertion are affirmed! Knowing they must embrace those strengths, women are, at the same time, aware that they do
not represent the end point of the journey. These women can see that
when men leave out Receiving, they leave out an essential dimension of
life. At the same time men who have achieved some confidence in their
power are learning to put it at the service of others and to welcome
women as their colleagues. And so we arrive at a dialectical movement

in which men develop a listening ear and women gain a voice. Women and men will benefit from paying attention to the way the other sex inhabits Integrated authority, because these pictures let us see people doing wonderful things with what's likely to be our own problem area. Here we have important gifts to offer each other.

This new paradoxical relationship between women and men means that the tensions are now *within* them—not *between* them. We no longer count on those others—men or women—to represent the unclaimed territory in our own hearts; instead we now stake our own claim on that wholeness for which we formerly depended on the other. Women move from "They know" to "I know" and then come to know that both are true. Men move beyond "power against" or "power over" to reclaim a receptive posture from which they can exercise power for and with others. As we move beyond control and passivity, we can also join our wish to be Autonomous and our wish to connect with others. Women are no longer stuck in giving up their space; men are no longer stuck in the compulsion to grab all the space. We discover the possibility of embracing both self-definition and self-emptying. As we overcome the contradiction between active and receptive postures, we can heal the split be-tween doing and being-in-relationship, between task and people, between work and love.

As we seek a vision of the partnership of women and men in the church, we may now take as our text "...neither male nor female." We can, for example, bring our different styles of evoking the authority of others and come very near each other. Jim Adams evokes the authority of others through modeling self-definition while letting go control. From a position alongside her parishioners Dorothy McMahon brings her evocative posture: "...when I preach, nearly all my sermons come from my relationships of the week...and I always feel as though the people have *given* me my sermons and I have the gift to articulate what it is that we've experienced together. The agenda of our parish is not mine, ever, and I'm always grateful that it isn't."

Women who have discovered their authority and men who have discovered that authority doesn't mean getting your own way can now work as partners. The hostility that had been the external sign of the conflict within us has now been broken down. And now the authority toward which men and women have struggled in their own ways finds its foundation within the community.

To conclude this chapter, here is a story that paints a picture of a new beginning at an ending—the story of how the church began, with a man and a woman. John, who always looks back behind the beginnings everyone else sees, here tells the story of Mary and the beloved disciple being given to each other at the foot of the cross. (19:25-27) With the words "Woman, here is your son," we see a woman and a man being brought together in a new family—just at the moment each is left alone.

This story of a new beginning starts by the cross: the last place we would think of—right in the midst of defeat, murder, and smashed hopes. (Yet, when we pause to reflect more deeply, it is the first place we would think of.) In the midst of the pangs of death, Jesus announces the birth of the church. This new beginning is intimately related to the ending. Jesus is going away. While he was present in the flesh, his friends could not fully accept their authority. Until the body of Christ was laid to rest they could not be the body of Christ.

Notice that the first two people in the newborn church are a man and a woman—perhaps the two people who loved him most. But this new family is a mother and a son, rather than a family that finds its beginning in a sexual relationship. And it is a mother and a son joined, not by bonds of blood, but by the love of Christ. This germ of a family, a woman and a man, is uniquely the family that will be able to welcome in more and more family members. It is a family that can even reach out to embrace the whole world.

Reflecting on your own experience:

Look back at the sections you have underlined or highlighted—places where you responded, "Yes, this is true for me." Now review those passages with these questions:
    —Where have I been?
    —Where am I now?
    —What invites me into my next stage of growth in authority?
Now go back and underline or highlight in a different color whatever strikes you as important to you about the dynamics of the other sex. What helps illuminate your understanding of men or women who are significant in your life? What seems important as you seek to make sense of your own development against the background of your picture of the others (women or men)?

CHAPTER V

The Paradoxical Authority of Laity and Clergy

Just as half the interviewees were men and half women, there were an equal number of parish clergy and laity with a clear consciousness of moving out in ministry on Monday mornings. I asked them, "What's special about your authority as an ordained person or a lay person?" Their responses wove the stories of lay and ordained ministry in this chapter.

In the pulpit and by the family bathtub, in meetings at the U. S. Department of Labor and at First Baptist Church, we see portraits of authority in action—the kind of authority that transcends control. People who care most about keeping things under control don't trust that things will be all right if they leave any unaccounted-for spaces. But through the contradictions and tensions that Integrated authority allows, spaces do emerge—spaces full of unexpected promise.

Those tensive and paradoxical places where grace breaks through shine forth at many points in these stories of ministry. So we will use paradox as the primary lens for examining the authority of clergy and laity in the daily events of parish life and worldly occupations. And along the way there will also emerge other signs of Integrated authority, which we will lift up at the end of the chapter.

The Authority of Laity

First we'll hear some stories about the ministry of laity in the world—in the workplace and at home, and then we'll look at lay ministry in the church.

"I'm called to act my ministry out in God's world."

Judith McMorland: "In my classroom...that's where my ministry is."

Judith McMorland teaches personnel management and organizational change in the University of Auckland's continuing education program. In the classroom, she invites her students to share her authority and vision and welcomes their challenges: "Students say, 'Judith, this is a lot of bullshit!'" She laughs: "I ask them for a different explanation." Respectfully, she invites the students to own their authority: "I say 'I'll take every bit of power you'll give me, and you've got to learn not to give me your power.'" Her evocative, confrontive approach reminds me of a mother lion teaching her cubs to hunt!

Judith places a high value on her ministry in the classroom and on being a lay person. "I think we're very special! It's hard to put it into words, but I feel that we *are* the church and really without us there is no church, so I celebrate the fact that I'm a lay person... People have said, 'Are you ever going to be ordained?' and I've said, '*No*, that's *not* what I want to do. I'm a very good teacher and I love to teach...'" Judith would like the church "to value that you can have a dynamic ministry in the classroom just as much as you do in the parish pew. Because actually I feel I do my work in my classroom. That's where my ministry is."

Judith McMorland and Keith Mason: at home, with the children

A couple of the interviewees, who exercise their authority with relative comfort in the workplace, encounter painful dilemmas as parents. Judith McMorland's "mother lion" confrontations with her students contrast with her experience at home. In the classroom, this "feels fine. It doesn't feel fine when my son says no." "You can be professionally very laid back; my experience is I can handle that very, very well;" but "I can't handle my son saying 'Get knotted!' ... It is hard...I burst into tears or I sort of go away and think about things for a while." But "there is such a strong bond between us that those are very surface things, and so we've never been in a situation where we can't simultaneously say, 'I'm sorry.'"

Keith Mason, Solicitor General of New South Wales, also finds authority more difficult to exercise at home:

"When I'm at work, I say, 'Let it be done,' and it gets done. I can't get my five-year-old to go get into the bath when it's time for the bath. I regard parenting as the most challenging and difficult task I've ever embarked on. And I suppose in part it's because kids aren't programmed into accepting authority. If you think authority is a good thing or if you are intent on establishing it within the family, you've got to work on it, and I suppose I've never been happy with direct exercise of authority... the tension is between going along with the child because you think that's the loving thing to do, and then saying, 'No—and you'll get a smack if you don't do it,' and suddenly reverting from the friend to the authority figure.

"If you have a vision of what you'll achieve with a happy, rounded child growing up, you have to struggle along the way with taking roles that don't seem natural... One of the lessons my wife and I have tried to teach each other is not to make too much of an issue over certain things because the danger is always that the ultimate issue becomes your authority rather than the task at hand or the long-term happiness of the unit or of the child." While at times the issue seemed to be, "'Look, who's in charge?' ...I feel that was not what was really at stake..."

As a father, Keith Mason may have to assert his authority to retain it; but if he does so he runs the risk that his authority will be seen as central when he knows it's not. These dilemmas with our children seem to lead us, not toward solutions, but deeper into the mystery at the heart of life.

Ruth Shinn: Poised between transcendent and proximate sources of authority in the U.S. Department of Labor

As Chief of the Division of Legislative Analysis in the Women's Bureau of the U. S. Department of Labor, Ruth Shinn finds herself living between two kinds of authority—"one in the global or religious context: I feel called to—at the very least—love and justice. But I don't feel told to do a particular thing by God" at a particular moment.

The other kind of authority arises because "human beings get together and create nations or institutions. They make compacts with each

other, and within those compacts they establish rules... Sometimes
there's a clash...take the Birmingham bus boycott—there's a time to
challenge one kind of authority because you feel the compelling force of
the call for justice. My response to what I recognize as compelling in the
universe might call me to challenge an agreed-upon authority... If any of
these human-made compacts become too far out of line, then either I
need to change them or leave the group. ...Otherwise I would feel a
pretty high sense of responsibility to move along with the agreed-upon
authority. I don't casually criticize."

Ruth frequently experiences the squeeze between transcendent
values and human rules not only in her work situation but *within herself.*
She *is* the interface between the hierarchy of her agency and her staff
members who want to challenge its authority. Although she tries hard to
pay attention to the people, she knows her staff sees her as task-oriented.
"And I lean to complying with the authority above me, and the people on
the staff team that I lead would much more often want me to challenge
the authority.

"They challenge me and challenge me: 'Well, why do we have to
do that?' all the time. Well, there are times that I can carry their challenge on up the line, and there are times that it seems to me so utterly
fruitless to do that [that I think,] 'Well, why are we spending time talking
about it?'...I think it's possible that I want so badly to be democratic or
fair that they feel a tentativeness in my exercising authority and they
manipulate that."

Although she works in a hierarchy where higher-ups call the shots
and lower-downs obey, Ruth Shinn's values lead her to want to collaborate. Instead of challenging the system directly, however, she prefers to
look for opportunities to modify it: "If there are parameters within which
we are working, I announce them: 'This product is due Friday noon.'
But very often there are situations where we can decide how we want to
do something and which persons are going to accept which tasks, and I
do not start by giving my opinion in that instance, I invite comment...
We're rotating chairing my staff meeting. There are four of us, two pro-
fessionals and a secretary and myself, and I chair one of four times. I
feel that they like it and do it well: the secretary is perfectly able to chair
the meeting, and now she wants to join a toastmaster's club and learn to
do public speaking. I was pleased with that. So I've tried to loosen
things up.

"But if someone else is chairing and people are saying, 'Well, let's decide not to have this project due at noon on Friday, then I would play my authoritarian role and say 'The Secretary of Labor wants it at noon on Friday. She's going to Canada and that's when her plane leaves.'"

Ruth keeps struggling with the conflict between her values and bureaucratic reality. "Government...is indeed hierarchic, and you can do things like rotating leadership in the staff meeting to make it less tightly hierarchical, but the fact is, if something is written by this staff person, everybody on up the line has to sign off... If you think the product just isn't good and you know what the next person is expecting, and you know absolutely that person is going to shoot it down, then you say to yourself, '*I'd* better shoot it down.' Then you go back and say to the staff member, 'You know, this really needs to be put in different terms.'"

Thinking through the conflict. "There are times when my vision is different from my superior's, but I know that...their boss won the election and under our system they have the right to pursue the policies they're pursuing. I give input and technical support...in the direction of what I want to do, but if they want to do something different I have to prepare support material for that. I've thought that one through very carefully, and I can live with that because I do believe in a two-party system. And if you're going to have political appointees and civil servants (and I think you need civil servants in a system—you'd have chaos if you changed everybody in all the agencies) you've got to agree to [support positions that are not your own.]"

How can she live with that conflict?

"Sometimes you give things a nudge, and sometimes you improve things along the way. I think you *can* make incremental differences, and so that's one reason I stay inside the system. Otherwise you stay outside the system and complain about it and bang on the table."

Ruth Shinn does not typically experience the call to stand over against the system that we will shortly encounter in Keith Mason. She just searches out opportunities to live by her transcendent values. "Even in a hierarchy sometimes I think you can do things to free people."

A number of factors facilitate her friendly, negotiating posture toward the authorities she encounters in her daily work. The U. S. Department of Labor is, to some degree at least, responsive to her initiatives for change. She is a basically optimistic person with a "can do" attitude nourished by years of experiencing that she is, indeed, able to make a difference. At times, of course, her initiatives fail. And then she is willing to challenge when necessary, to negotiate and accommodate where she can. She is willing to take the poor fit between ideals and opportunities into herself and live with it if that seems the best alternative. She finds the disjunctures between the powers in the system and the transcendent call manageable more often than not. And so, though there is no neat fit, Ruth Shinn works at discovering ways to find some accommodation between the basic realities in her life: her values and her workplace, as well as the church she attends on Sundays, which she finds supportive of the values she seeks to realize Mondays at the office.

Hold Ruth Shinn, as she struggles with the disjunctures between those two worlds, in your mind, as we move on to look at others' experiences with struggles and disjunctures. We will now hear from some laity who find themselves caught between those realities at work, and then from those who discover they are called to be prophets in the church.

Richard Tustian and Peter Sherer: hard places at work

I kept noticing a "bottom line" in lay people's stories about their work. They seemed more often to live on the "hard edges." When faced with choices between results and personnel, in the end they were required to do what it took to get the job done.

Richard Tustian, out of his experience as a land use planner and his attempt to make sense of it through organizational theory, made a distinction between "command" and "nurture" organizations that helped me understand these "rocks" in the lay workplace. Though he regretted the necessity, when it came to the bottom line in a command organization, Tustian was forced to place a higher value on production than people.

Peter Sherer also acknowledged that his role held the possibility of requiring him to choose results over people. "It's more than a possibility. I crushed people in my role as a bureaucrat. I had the responsibility to worry about the performance of people who worked for me and weren't measuring up. A man ten years my senior with two children dependent on him—I drummed him out of the service. It was an incredibly painful thing to do." "How do you respond when you find yourself in that bind?" I asked. "The typical way is to look all over the place for a bargain. A way to minimize the steam roller effect of the institution on the person... What systems can I put in place to minimize the damage? Then I just act, remembering I am a human being. The role does have its demands. I'm being required to act."

Clergy work in "nurture" organizations. Perceptive pastors like the interviewees in this study know their task is to nurture-into-being a community that supports people's spiritual growth. The church's "product" is transformed people. So that agonizing choice between product and people is not built into the clergy job as inescapably as it is for the lay person who works in a "command" organization. (Of course, some lay people also work in "nurture" organizations: teachers' and consultants' jobs resemble clergy roles in this way more than they resemble the legal system or the U.S. Department of Labor.) This distinction can help clergy listen to laity and respect this typical difference between the demands of their workplaces.

The Authority of the Laity in the Church

Lay people report a variety of experiences when they attempt to exercise their authority in church. Some find they do have some authority within a church setting, and others find that they do not.

Richard Tustian replied: "Well, as a layman you don't exercise any authority in the church, do you?" He hears and accepts the message the church usually sends: "You have no authority here."

Keith Mason: a Lay Prophet to the Church

Keith Mason is a good example of a layman who, instead of assenting to the church hierarchy's message "You have no authority," asserts his authority with confidence.
Hahn: "Is there anything special about the way you exercise your authority that's unique to being a layman?"
Mason: "Well, of course in church matters I'm a layman, in legal matters I'm a cleric."
This fragment of our interview left me with an uncomfortable recognition that my own ecclesiastical preconceptions had been exposed: I had come to our conversation with an assumption that the church was the

Real World. Mason let me know, not only that he has authority in the legal profession, but that, as he went on to say, the lay person is "the voice of what the real church is all about." The church says "you have no authority." But Keith Mason responds "Yes I do!"

Keith Mason is convinced that "Church ought to be concerned with life"—therefore he's willing to be "a nuisance." The diocese of Sydney holds that "ordination confers an authority and a recognition that you are speaking for the capital 'C' Church or the official church. I see all lay authority as having to struggle against that in order to make the point that the church is wider than that. We are all in one church... Now a lay person just doesn't start off with any authority conferred by the church, but the lay person is the voice of what the real church is all about. Church ought to be concerned with life. What we're really fighting about is what the real church is all about... My struggles within the church have taught me that authority consists in part of my hope of resisting the blandishments and being prepared to just make a nuisance of myself..."

Laity as Prophets

Both Ruth Shinn and Keith Mason find themselves struggling to realize transcendent values in the situation right under their noses. We've focused here on Keith Mason's collision with the church, and we've examined Ruth Shinn's quest for opportunities to incarnate her values in the U. S. Department of Labor. It is the perceived disjuncture between the divine imperative and the daily task that issues in the prophetic call. Laity are best positioned to notice where a worldly institution fails to carry out its life and work according to the values of love and justice. Unlike clergy, who don't bump up against the world's systems on a daily, sustained basis, laity do live in the world, encounter worldly "powers that be" daily, and receive daily opportunities to examine those powers by the light of their religious values.

Laity occupy a similarly tensive position in relation to the church. Lay people like Mason, McMorland, and Shinn say "We *are* the church," but they don't run it. These prophets who demand a church that is relevant to real life in the world naturally spring from the group who have enough distance from the ecclesiastical institution and enough presence in society to protest the ways in which the world is not being served.

The role of prophet requires a capacity for autonomous leadership grounded in a vision of God's will, a willingness to exercise authority as over-againstness when necessary. Thus Keith Mason is prepared to make "a nuisance" of himself, and Judith McMorland to be "very rude about the clergy." From that uncomfortable space between the powers-that-be and a vision of God's truth, these self-differentiated, autonomous leaders provide a gift for us all as they clarify the choices that they—and we—must make.

Some lay people, like Richard Tustian, hear and accept the message that they have no authority in the church. Others, like Mason, energetically reject that message. And still others, like Ruth Shinn, choose and relish church settings where their authority is welcomed.

Ruth Shinn: Sharing Ministry in the Church

After struggling all week to find spaces for love, justice, and collaboration at the Department of Labor, Ruth finds a welcome congruence between institution and values at First Congregational Church in downtown Washington. As a leader in First Church, "...you're a *moderator*, you're not a president or a director... And the moderator's role in the agreed-upon rules is to free the group to come to its decision, and that I enjoy very much. I....never felt really any conflict about authority in church leadership. I do believe very much in the ministry of all the people of God... I don't see any line between membership and ministry."

Foundations of lay authority

Two interviewees' comments provide further clarity. What are the foundations of lay authority? Verna Dozier replied immediately: "That's what's special about [my authority]: It doesn't come from any institution." She is independent. A free-lance Christian. And that is what distinguishes her from the clergy. Colin Bradford's reply points to the other foundation of lay authority: "My authority...is much more based on my *experience* and how I would tend to handle things than it is on...any formal knowledge base..."

Colin's authority goes into action where the rubber hits the road. Like all lay Christians, he is out in the world living on the boundary between God's call and the requirements of the situation immediately in front of him, forging out his responses moment by moment.

Clergy often assume a bipolar perspective:

CHURCH/ GOD	WORLD/Home, Work, Community

Laity are often clearer that they live in the space between three realities:

	GOD	
WORLD/Home, Work, Community		**CHURCH**

They are attempting to live in the world according to God's call. While for many of them, the church clearly stands under judgment, I hear them *wanting* to be supported by the church. Judith McMorland says, "I would love the church...to value that you can have a dynamic ministry in the classroom just as much as you do in the parish pew." When the church refuses to hear their voices, laity have to challenge the church.

The church clearly blesses the clergy's authority, but what does the church do for lay people's authority? Tipping our hat toward the authority of the laity by commissioning them in ministries, using the ordination of clergy as a model, does not constitute an adequate response. We need to look at how we can support lay authority more effectively.

The church must begin with the recognition that it does not know the answers to the world's problems, and that it does not own God for lay people. Relinquishing any claim to be a Control church, church leaders need to recognize that God is already with lay people out in the world where they carry out their "ministries." (And we probably need to find another less ecclesiastical word.) How do church leaders effectively support laity as they live in "the space" described above? To that question we will shortly turn.

Arena or Status?

Let's address this question first, however: Is the ministry of the laity distinguished from that of the clergy by arena or status?

Here is another interview fragment that surfaced a disagreement worth examining. About her pastor, Joyce Yarrow confidently asserted: "Through Dee Crabtree's leadership and her sharing authority with us, we know we are all ministers." Ministry happens in "day-to-day activities." I asked Joyce whether "the difference between your authority as a lay person and Dee's authority as a clergy person might be that you exercise authority primarily in a worldly arena?" She replied, "I don't think I agree... I'm called to act it out in a total arena, God's world, as I believe an ordained person is..."

"So you want to emphasize what's the *same* in your ministries?" I inquired. Joyce's answer: "I have often said to Dee that in her role as ordained minister or pastor she is...a cut above the rest of us... [An ordained minister's] "call is a little bit more special because it's a spiritual leadership."

Since Joyce Yarrow doesn't want to distinguish clergy and laity by the arenas of their ministry, she falls back on distinguishing them by saying that her minister is "a cut above"—even though both Joyce and Dee come from the U.C.C. tradition and stress their egalitarian views about church roles! This time the conversation reinforced my own sense that a more useful distinction is made between the world as the primary place where the ministry of the laity is carried out and the church as the primary setting for clergy ministry.

Ministry in the world...ministry in the church: What's the connection?

What is the relationship between these two places where ministry is carried out—the church and the world? When the connections between what we do in church and what we do every day aren't clear, we get into trouble.

If lay people are out on the front lines at the Department of Labor (or the Law Review Commission or the National Community AIDS Partnership) slogging away at difficult tasks without any equipping or encouragement, that's a serious problem.

If lay people are nestled into their cozy parish churches, busying themselves with church committee meetings while ignoring worldly dilemmas, we have another kind of problem.

And if clergy have all the authority in the church, still another problem arises, for then lay people will not be helped to develop confidence in their own authority as ministers and theologians in the world.

If churches want to take seriously their role of equipping the saints for their ministries in the world, the most useful way for them to do that will be to reframe church activities as laboratories in which laity are encouraged to own their authority, explore the connections between sacred lore and daily experience, and practice making decisions that join the transcendent call with the practical requirements of the moment. When church is seen "as a place where you get to practice what it means to be human,"[1] what goes on in the church and what goes on in the world are usefully connected.

We need places where it's safe to practice. It's hard to risk trying out new behavior amid all the principalities and powers in the federal government or a huge corporation. There's too much at stake. And in the family, too, the stakes are too high for practicing. In addition, relationships are so emotionally loaded that conflicts become more agonizing still, and it's hard to get enough distance and perspective to try new behavior.

We also need shared authority and ministry in the congregation so that laity can be, not just passive receivers, but active experimenters. When lay people collaborate in designing and carrying out worship and education, those enterprises will be relevant to the daily lives of the people who are worshipping and learning. In such a laboratory, ministry in the church and ministry in the world can be held together in a way that helps send laity back out into their world empowered for those paradoxical places in which they are called to stand.

The Authority of Clergy

We began this exploration with a consideration of the situation of lay people because it is with lay people that clergy are called to work. In speaking about laity, therefore, we have already begun to outline the challenge clergy face as they seek to exercise *their* authority. How do faithful and competent ordained ministers perform their task of equipping the worldly saints who carry out their ministries suspended between the transcendent and the proximate? How do those ordained ministers call into being a community where everybody's authority is enhanced? And how do they hold their ministries open to God (as distinguished from identifying them with God)?

Let's look at some more portraits—this time of several clergy, each of whom has found a distinctive way to shape the ordained leader's role toward those purposes.

Jim Adams: Authenticity

For James R. Adams, rector of a 900 member Episcopal church on Capitol Hill in Washington, D.C., authority comes from being "real." "For me, my authority is my capacity to be what I consider authentic, saying what I really think and feel. I have authority if what I do and say has some congruence with what's really going on in me."

Adams thus takes pains to define himself and his position honestly, and this self-differentiation invites the self-differentiation of others. He has found that stating his own opinion helps others clarify where they stand. When he kept his own opinions to himself in order to provide opportunities for parishioners to clarify their own thinking, church members said they saw his behavior as "contemptuous." It was as though if he said what he thought on the matter, others would be forced to knuckle under and agree. Having been taught this lesson by his vestry, Adams says, "Now, as soon as I have a position, I try to state it calmly as just my opinion. Then I try to detach myself emotionally from my position so that other people can sharpen what they think."

Cherishing his own inner integrity and comfortable with differences, Adams handles conflict with relative equanimity. His difficulty arises not in defining himself but in getting alongside his parishioners.

A recent weekend conference led by lay codirectors of Christian education confirmed his instinct that revealing his own blunders is an effective
strategy for reaching toward identity with others.

> Both in trying to rescue [the weekend] and in the means of rescue, I
> made some errors... Having openly blundered I found that I got a
> whole lot more authority given to me by the people on the Christian
> education staff. They said, "Oh, he screws up, *too*. He's one of *us*."
> ...There is a kind of authority that comes from people saying, 'You
> are one of us.' I think Jesus must have had both. I was always
> taught that he became one of us and yet was different. I err on the
> side of remoteness because of my personality... That's why in
> preaching I frequently try to find illustrations in which my ineptness
> can be held up to laughter.

As he reflects on this weekend drama, we can see Adams working with
the tension between separation, which comes easily to him, and identification, for which he must struggle.

Adams rejects the idea that authority means exerting power over
others. Observing colleagues in conflict with their congregations who
"start talking about 'their authority as the priest and the rector,'" Adams
says, "I know they are in trouble. If what you rely on to get things done
is role authority, you are becoming oppressive, and you are going to get a
negative and hostile reaction."

In his own parish as well, Adams has experienced that pushing
elicits a negative reaction. "Since 1972 I have wanted to get the en-
trances of this church to be more inviting [by putting in glass doors], but
every time I push it nothing happens. I just get into a fight with people
because it's not something that other people think is important." "I can't
control their reactions," he concludes. Instead, "My style leans toward
[supporting the people I'm working with.] There are very few tasks that
I can think of that are so important that I have to get them done. When I
primarily support people, then lots gets done, but it may not be exactly
what I had in mind."

Anyhow, he has concluded that goals in themselves are ambiguous.
When he gets attached to them, it just causes trouble. "In moments of
grace," he concludes, "sometimes I am able to withhold my attempts at
controlling life and trying to be somebody."

And paradoxically, when he doesn't push his authority, parishioners are more likely to give it to him. "Because I don't exert it institutionally I think people are more willing to hand it to me."

Wanting to give others the freedom and respect that are so important for him, Adams supports laity in owning their authority. He refuses to be their authority so they can find their own.

> People don't work on their own authority until they are willing to withdraw what they are inappropriately projecting onto me...I try to use the perception of divine authority responsibly and give people their religious authority back... There aren't any answers that we can give them. They have to find their own answers for them to have any meaning in their lives. But no matter what we do, there are people who want to give the leaders their authority instead of claiming it for themselves. Part of our educational discipline is to refuse to be their authority so that they can find their own...I have *my* answers. I know what works for me, but I can't hand my answers to other people, or I'll still be their authority... In the unfolding story [of Jesus] we can see the way the disciples discovered their own authority in spite of themselves because Jesus refused to be the answer for them. That's the best model I know.

Adams takes obvious pleasure in cleverly arranging situations in which lay leaders can take authority. One year the Every Member Canvass was obviously not working. Adams called a meeting, at the end of which, he recalls: "I said that we need to transfer the authority to the lay leadership." The whole process was carried out "so adroitly that nobody noticed... They felt empowered because I was there backing them up. That's the way I like to use authority."

Adams is an Autonomous leader. He rigorously monitors his authenticity: What do I stand for? Is that the way I'm behaving? Self-differentiation is like breathing for him; it's staying in touch that requires hard work. He is clear that he does not want to achieve connection through controlling other people or trying to sell them his own answers. Instead he reveals his clay feet as one who "screws up" and he refuses to provide answers about the meaning of life even when his refusal enrages would-be disciples. Adams offers others what he values so much for himself: the opportunity to define themselves. "You have your own authority," he tells them in every way he can. People's experiences at St. Mark's are designed to help them grow confident enough of their authority that they will move out to families and offices ready to carry out their ministries there with boldness.

Jim Adams' ministry is friendly with paradox, with its mysterious open space—a space out of which authority and ministry are born.

Dee Crabtree: The Coach

Is it time to move to two Sunday morning services? As Senior Minister Davida Crabtree and the members of Colchester Church worked through that question, their process had the flow of a dance: one partner steps forward, the other steps back; they take turns and then pause for an intermission. Dee tells the story:

> When...our church was at the point at which it needed to move to two services, it was also clear to me that I had the authority to introduce the notion. It never occurred to me to simply say "We will do this now"—but to introduce the notion and get people talking about it. When it became clear to me that...there was resistance... I then used my authority to say, "We're not going to talk about this right now. We are going to back off"...and that was a fairly clear use of authority, but one that—probably because it was authority very much in line with what people wanted—was very easily accepted.

Notice how Dee Crabtree initiates the "free-form choreography": she puts forward the question about two services and encourages discussion. This open invitation invites collaboration in the way that a complete up-front strategy could never do.

An integration of leader, community, and God

Dee Crabtree experiences her authority not as over against the congregation but as integrated with the people, with what is going on in the church, and with their mutual attempts to listen for where God wants them to go. "...I experience that process as a very deeply spiritual one...integrating within me all of what's happening around. Yet at the same time it's not least common denominator politics."

The vertical dimension moves right through the process. "My experience of God in the midst of that process is within the community and within my own process. So I don't think of God as an external source of authority at all."

At times, all that is going on in and around Dee is so thoroughly integrated that she takes action without a pause for deliberation. At the 1969 NCC General Assembly, a powerful presentation by James Foreman was immediately followed by a conventional progression to the "order of the day." "I never asked myself whether I could do it. I was just *propelled* to the microphone: 'What day is this? What order are we talking about? Are we not going to respond?'" This immediate action is typical for Dee: she engages fully in the moment, ready to turn on a dime. The process flows.

The pastor's vision is connected to the people's lives. "I think the secret is not in choosing *whether* to introduce a vision. The secret is almost always in *how*." As minister of the Colchester church, Dee saw her job as "coach" to be helping the people "discover the authority of their own lives and the possible ministries that they might have." She found ways to introduce "the ministry of the laity in such a way...that it would fit with their culture, with their understanding and could then begin to stretch them." Because the minister and her vision are not defined in opposition to the people, the vision is less likely to provoke negative reaction.

Authority is thus mutual and evocative. "I try to enable the group to claim *its* authority rather than my claiming authority." "The community grants me that authority partly because I never violate their granting of it." We can see the results of this mutual exercise of authority in a period of parish conflict, when, because of her collaborative style, "I wasn't hanging out there alone. It was 'us.' It wasn't me against the world."

Dee's passion for the authority and ministry of the laity means that she doesn't operate out of any assumption that her ministerial authority is special. "I really believe that baptism is the true ordination and that as an ordained person I am set in the midst of people to serve them and to lead them and that my authority...is not significantly different than [church member] Gary's authority as a database administrator...I don't think that God has put a special halo around my authority in relation to laity." She is convinced "that the only way we can equip the saints is to *honor* them as saints."

As pastor, what does Dee Crabtree *do* to invite this integration of authority between herself and her parishioners? In meetings, says Dee, "I usually say what I think. But I try to do that in a way that invites them into dialogue...I work very hard not to do that at times when it's strategic that I *not* do it, but my impulse is very clearly to, sometime in the first ten or fifteen minutes, get it out there."

In counseling, "I become a mirror and they become able to see themselves with greater clarity because I have stayed clear...if I back away from...moments of conflict I miss some of the greatest opportunities with people. [In those conflictual encounters,] I'm like a board... If I am willing to stand there and let them hit up against me for a while... then it does shift to a mirror and people are able to make many more breakthroughs in their own lives."

The mutuality between pastor and people is fed by her willingness to receive from the people as well as give to them. Dee described a difficult situation that arose after the church decided to manage its investments according to criteria shaped by a commitment to social responsibility. After the church voted not to invest in companies doing business with South Africa, Dee discovered that the committee chair had chosen an investment manager whose commitment to that decision was limited to simple adherence to the Sullivan principles. What should she do? The committee had been entrusted with the responsibility, but as Dee saw it, that responsibility was not being exercised in accordance with the vote taken by the congregation. She went to the Diaconate and said: "I need to ask for your wisdom on how I should handle this...I don't ever want to be a person who undermines the work of a committee in the life of the church. On the other hand I have a responsibility as a leader and a responsibility to the church which has voted something different than [what] this committee is coming in to recommend. I am really caught between a rock and a hard place. And I need your wisdom...I am not sharing this with you because I want Diaconate to take an action. I am sharing it with you as your pastor because I personally need your wisdom." At the end of the story of this dilemma about managing investments, concluded Dee, "It's all come out okay."

Dee receives not only advice but affirmation from her parishioners. Their grateful notes buoy her up at hard moments.

What's the downside in this picture of a pastor's authority?

Dee Crabtree's temptation is just the opposite of some other interviewees: for her, Autonomy is the weak place in her integration. Under fire she can be tempted to dispense with her authority. She finds herself saying, "'Oh, well, of course he knows what he's talking about.' And I have to really maintain strong discipline in myself to bring myself to speak up in those situations where my view is different."

Dee Crabtree's style is integrative and collaborative. She is set in the midst of the people, working out of a vision in which God, the people, and her own initiatives move together like a dance. Her authority is not that of one set apart or set over; instead it takes its shape as she invites all those dimensions of life into a living unity.

These stories succeed one another in a contrapuntal pattern. Crabtree's path as pastor moves in the opposite direction from that of Jim Adams, who, rooted firmly in his own Autonomy, had to work hard to connect with others. In contrast, Dee Crabtree is so open to the whole situation around her that she faces the danger of *losing herself*, abandoning confidence in her own unique point of view. Under stress, she has to fight not to relinquish her Autonomy.

On the sidelines

For a pastor with these strengths and this struggle, the "coach on the sidelines" is a model that fits. "Coaching" as a style says the action takes place somewhere else, not in the church. The coach backs off and then the players do their real work. If we are to be "imitators of God," as the author of Ephesians puts it, perhaps "coach" is an apt metaphor for the authority of a God who invites, cares, guides, but also offers freedom and respect. Friedman recalls a Hebrew word that says God "shrinks" to provide free space for the human players.[2]

Dee's authority is a good imitation; it aims to enhance her parishioners' ministry in the world. Her vision is "tailored" to the people's lives. She equips the saints by *honoring* them, by making the concerns of laity the church's agenda. In her book *The Empowering Church*, she describes how Colchester's whole parish structure was reshaped so that it actually supported the ministry of the laity in the world.

And so Dee Crabtree both honors and equips the laity, affirming their authority in the process and structure of the congregation. Placing her gift for integration at the service of parish life, she points the way for laity to listen, through corporate life and leadership dilemmas, for the leadings of God.

Dwight Lundgren: The Robe—symbol of the clergy role

Every Sunday Dwight Lundgren, Senior Minister of First Baptist Church in Providence, Rhode Island, dons his robe—a robe with a paradoxical meaning. It stands for his seminary training and professional expertise. It also signals that "we're all fools for Christ," dressing up to play a game. "Fools." "Game." Words with a lightness that skitters off beyond their literal meaning. Let's look first at the role symbolized by Lundgren's ministerial robe.

The Role

Role means first that you're hired to do a job. "And so there is the authority that they...extend to you based on the role that you've entered into... You sit at the middle of a communications network, and you are the gatekeeper."

What you do is shaped more by the job's requirements than by personal inclination. "I am the facilitator of the strange process that we call the coming-into-being-of-a-community, that we call a congregation. I'm kind of a servant of that. And that's what I mean by 'the authority comes from the role'... It's not *my* congregation. *They're* the congregation: 'You're paying me to do this.'"

Dwight is clear that his *self* is distinct from his *role*. "I'm comfortable with myself and understand the limits of who I am and what I do, and that who I am is not coterminous with my role as a minister... I'm more than a minister and I'm also less than a minister... And that allows them to be who they are also."

Lundgren has a very human-sized view of his role. I sense expectancy in him and also a contented recognition that there's nothing flashy or glorious about that role. In fact, many people look upon being a minister as a questionable sort of career: "I remember this friend in college who, when he heard I was going to seminary, was horrified, and he came up to me and with all genuineness he said, 'Why are you doing this? You're throwing your life away...' And I even put him off dishonestly by saying, 'Well, I'm going to teach religion in college.' 'Oh, well, that's different. That's respectable...' I don't tell people until it's absolutely necessary that I'm a minister...because it always screws things up..." In parish life, Lundgren makes choices that communicate his human-sized picture of his role. "When Kate came we agreed she was not going to be associate, she was not assistant, we are colleagues. And some of the nice moments are when people say to us 'You know, we really like the way you interact'... We share the preaching equally because we wanted to model this for people."

The robe represents expertise

Lundgren's open, hospitable expertise also conveys the message, "this is not my congregation." For example, this pastor, trained in exegesis and homiletics, wants to preach in a way that helps parishioners "feel comfortable handling [scripture] themselves, so that they feel as I'm working in it, 'Oh *that's* how you do that.' It's not that I just come with the meaning, but I come showing how I got there..." Part of the skill of preaching is finding ways to evoke the theological authority of the people sitting in pews.

...And the robe hints that 'we're all fools for Christ'

Expertise in exegesis: that we expect. But the robe also points in an opposite direction: "I think of myself as kind of a court jester and free lancer in life." This "fool" is always wondering about God. "Even if I weren't being paid to do this, I'd be sitting here wondering about God, thinking about these things and talking to people about them. They want someone who's doing that, you know, and coming back with a report once a week—'What's this all about?' ...Always wondering about God. Almost preoccupied with thinking about it and talking about it and trying to open up the scriptural warrants..." As one who wonders, Lundgren's selfhood and servanthood come together.

The lightness of Lundgren's style is a form of awe. "We're talking about God! What do we know about God? *We're* the ones who are saying [these things] and so we'd better be fairly light about it."

As "expert" makes way for "fool," we see Dwight Lundgren as the modest facilitator of a great spaciousness. There's no hint of messianism in this picture: "I've never had this sense that somehow I was God's person, and therefore these people were disappointing not only me, they were disappointing God Almighty in either the pace or the direction that things were going. I just think this is something that we are all in the midst of, and you celebrate what you can." Here's a pastor who is comfortable with his *limits*. These limits allow others to be who they are and also sketch the tenuous boundaries of open space for wondering about God.

The role: to be a host

Dwight Lundgren finds a model for his ministry in Barnabas, a "son of encouragement." "Barnabas in Acts is a very rich figure to me...the encourager and hospitality person, giving hospitality... Barnabas is the one who gets the church to accept Paul, give him a break... And he does that with Paul for Mark... 'Come on, bring the kid with us.'... A son of encouragement." Like Barnabas, Dwight has an important facilitating role, but he does not cast himself as one of the story's star actors.

Hospitality is not only a personal but also a corporate value. "We use the image of hospitality a lot... This church has a tradition of being open." Being hospitable to the whole person includes a willingness to postpone tasks for the sake of people. "We're always sensitive to 'Why is that person saying that, what's going on in their life at this point?'... So sometimes the agenda has to go.

This hospitality has a spacious, encouraging quality. I can't dictate another person's pilgrimage—where they are in life, what they're preoccupied with. I think of myself as someone who kind of hangs around people and at the appropriate providential time, when they're ready to talk about something and deal with it, we relate on a human level... You have to be happy with where people are at the moment, kind of celebrate what is being accomplished and then say, 'Well we don't have to stop here.'"

Open places emerge throughout the minister's role as shaped by

Lundgren. They break out as the paradox of role and selfhood—"I but not I." Lundgren's comfortable acceptance of the "*limits* of who I am and what I do" leaves space for God and for the people who come to First Baptist Church. The picture of the *humble leader* contains a pregnant ambiguity. The role as holding together "skills" and "fools" presents yet another paradox. The *skills* are roomy and hospitable, not an excluding sort of expertise, never a way to achieve control, but instead these are skills for letting people be where they are, and for enhancing their authority. At the same time they hold out the possibility of growth: "Well, we don't need to stop here." "Fools" suggests the lightness of a game or a dance—an open place that hints at awe.

Both as minister and as person, Dwight Lundgren's life is centered around the open space of "wondering," "not knowing." His willing acknowledgment that he does not know opens a door where mystery is welcomed in.

Dorothy McMahon—The Priest

"The priestly ministry is central to my understanding of what I'm doing," says Dorothy McMahon, Minister of Pitt Street Uniting Church in Sydney. For Dorothy, that ministry includes being humanly present to the people, staying open to God's grace, and bringing the sacraments to the people.

Moving toward claiming the priestly ministry

It was after many years as a key lay leader in her denomination that Dorothy McMahon decided to go to theological school and prepare for ordination. She told of gaining confidence through the women's movement, which, she said, "brought about a major transformation in my own self-awareness, my own confidence as a human being." She worked to gain the skills for this ministry, pursuing her natural gift for listening to people and learning alternatives to providing answers or just soaking up their pain like a blotter. She told of learning to accept the burden and constraints of leadership. Though she itched for the freedom to be "just a student," the Principal cautioned, "Your words have weight," and she learned leadership means "you don't just lightly say anything you feel like saying." And she learned to *take authority*:

"When I went into the ministry, in my first year or two I found myself uneasy about exercising authority at all. I believe the church and its ministry must face up to the responsibility of actually exercising authority. I understand that very much as authentically struggling to name the Word, to name what is the gospel for us at this moment—and a recognition that one will not always be right about that, by a long shot—that we see dimly. But to pull away from that is in fact to betray your calling and it often flows over into your pastoral work too where you hesitate to say, with great authority, that God is at the bottom of every abyss." Alongside the courage to claim authority stands a contrapuntal caution: "I sometimes experience in myself that inner authority which is of God, but I'm a bit wary of claiming that."

Being human

The first thing we have to say about Dorothy McMahon's authority as a priest is that it is grounded in her humanity.

Being with the people is central. In international meetings, postponing the customary task-oriented plunge into the agenda, Dorothy insisted that "we go around the room and get in touch with each other." First, "acknowledge who we are together in a caring and listening way—and then do the business."

Dorothy pays attention to being human with her people. She watches projections and counters them by "trying to establish a very human relationship with the people I'm working with." She keeps finding ways to contradict the image of lowly laity looking up at the Preacher on the Pedestal. "I reinforce people's awareness that they're not actually dependent on my presence. And I keep undermining that perception of who I am. I scrub the floor...I do flowers with the women..." Dorothy herself needs to be a human being alongside her parishioners: "If I have to be in a role, I am alienated and separated from people and I feel very lonely." And she is convinced that this human posture works for parishioners. "Parishes...can, in fact, cope with a person who is acknowledging very deep levels of humanness." "I'm fairly self-disclosing to significant bodies of people within the congregation."

Even when she was a child, Dorothy found that people kept telling her their life stories. "I began to be open to the possibility that if people were prepared to trust me with themselves, maybe there was some gift I had, maybe people felt in some way safe in telling me things. I regarded that as a sort of sacred trust, but also as a certain authority to take up my ministry." As she accepted "the authority of deeply connecting with the authentic feelings of people" she found alternatives to just absorbing people's pain or trying to solve their problems. But she held onto her conviction that these stories were gifts: "to hear things people are telling you—that is a...great privilege and honour."

In the same way, she experiences sermons as gifts; from this Integrated perspective on preaching, Dorothy sees her role as "to watch and listen and gather in and articulate." "Nearly all my sermons come from my relationships during the week, and I always feel as though the people have *given* me my sermons and my part is to articulate what it is that we've experienced together and bring the Word to bear on that."

The same sense of being *in* the situation with the people pervades Dorothy's perspective on discerning directions for parish life. "When I've had a clear and painful sense that the word that's being addressed to us is not one we want to hear... I've usually found that if I put it in those terms, the people will struggle with it. That it's the word *we* don't want to hear...I too sit under this...therefore it's with some pain and fear that I put it in front of us. I also think that some of our best moments in parish life have been when we think something has been asked of us from outside and we have had the guts to say to each other, 'We can't cope, so we'll have to say no.'"

We can see her central emphasis on staying human also in *exercising authority without dominating people.* You don't get authority from a role; it comes from that in a person which is "recognized as true and lifegiving. If I experience authority in another person, it's because my being leaps out towards that person and says, 'Oh, yes, I can see in you something that gives me life and truth.'" This authority is *Received*; it is "given to me by the community... At the beginning of one's ministry the church needs to say, 'We recognize and affirm something in you which indicates this vocation.' That's the authority to take up the task, but once I have taken up the task, I think I have authority only if I am genuinely being a minister of the word and sacrament. [Authority must be grounded in *Autonomy*.] That comes from an authentic struggle to understand what the Gospel is and to deliver the sacraments to the people."

Dorothy has learned through experience that authority is different from power. She had a chance to handle power, and gave it up. The experiments of her "power-tripping days" led her to the insight that authority comes from "authenticity without any strings or trickiness or jockeying for position—just straight authenticity." "Integrity has authority beyond anything that we can imagine." Change comes, not through the exercise of control, but through being human in the face of the vision.

This means that Dorothy's exercise of authority is collaborative. "What I am really trying to help them do is to claim their own authority." "The agenda of our parish is not mine, ever, and I'm always grateful that it isn't." At the close of a parish planning meeting, "Everybody has a sense of owning what we are trying to do."

Dorothy's most powerful sense of her authority emerges in vulnerable moments. With parish leaders, her failings provide openings. "I have responded very defensively sometimes and I have responded with hurt. And I've had to be challenged about those responses, too... And we've really gone through quite a painful and good process in working it through."

The sacraments are central

Dorothy describes her call to the sacramental ministry. Following the decision to lay down power, "I decided agonizingly that I shouldn't proceed to ordination. Having announced that to all and sundry, to everyone's distress, I felt absolutely desolate. I went into St. James' Anglican Church for communion, feeling just like a desert, dreadful. I went up to the communion rail to receive communion, and as the cup came into my hands there was a light around it. When the cup was taken on by the priest, the light stayed in my hands as I knelt there. And for a moment I had a sense of the cup being placed in my hands and of my having the authority to celebrate the sacraments. And after that I decided to proceed to ordination." "At my ordination, when I first celebrated, that moment was a moment of total personal integration I'd never experienced before, and that happens every time I celebrate the sacraments, so that there's something that becomes whole for me—I don't know what it is, I can't describe it."

Dorothy's posture as celebrant of the sacraments is a receptive one.

"I see myself as simply being a vehicle for [the Gospel]. It's rather like the sacraments—my hands just deliver them. The sacraments have nothing to do with my hands—they are the real presence of Jesus Christ. I am just there holding them with trust and faith, honoring the trust that has been placed in me by God and the people." She stands with the people. She brings the sacraments. She is a vehicle for the power that comes from beyond her. It's a human view, a low view, of her role.

She carries the sacraments to the oppressed. "Because I work with oppressed communities like the gay and lesbian community, Aboriginal community, Asian community and so on, people who are oppressed in this society, it is a great and amazing experience to carry the sacraments in to them and say, 'On the night he was *betrayed*, Jesus took bread...' What that does in that setting is just so special and so powerful that for me it is absolutely central to my ministry...I have a supply of pottery chalices, and at the ending of a marriage or some sense of deep sin or failure, having celebrated communion, at the end of the absolution, we take the cup, and we give it to the person and we say, 'Take this cup, and when you are tempted to believe that you are more human or less human than the rest of us, remember that we have shared the common cup with you.'"

This picture of sacramental ministry is full of paradox and open places. Sacraments and symbols, by their very nature, convey a tensive reality. They call the recipients to stand simply in their humanity and reject the temptations to opt out (you are not *more* human or *less* human). Sacraments open up for people the depths and the heights: "I think essentially (and it is linked with the sacraments) the concept of the brokenness and the paradoxical life and wholeness that flows out of that symbolizes virtually everything I've said. If I will present myself as the broken human being who bears witness with grateful heart to the grace of God and the life that can flow...out of that, and if I bear witness to how I see that happening in a group of people, it seems to me that's central to my authority and to what I understand it means to be a Christian. For me, the crucifixion-resurrection patterns of life are what it's all about. It's about entering into that brokenness in your own life and bearing witness that you may do that in safety. And that's what Jesus reveals— that life is more powerful than death and that we may safely enter every death, because Jesus has entered every death ahead of us and comes out full of life. It's the common cup, and the brokenness, and the wholeness, that I can't really go beyond."

I want to underline three themes in Dorothy McMahon's picture of her ministry. First, *her ministry is grounded in being human.* She is gentle with herself and she is gentle with others; listening to them is an "honor." Acknowledging "very deep levels of humanness" "prepares the ground" for accepting God's call. This "being human" has a porous, open quality.

Second, *she holds that being-human, that being-with-people, open to God's grace.* That conjunction of deep—and even broken—humanity and grace is at the core of her own experience. We see it in the picture of her coming into St. James' Church in a condition for which the words that come are "distress"..."desolate...desert...dreadful..." and being met by "light..." Therefore she can say to others with great conviction: "We may safely enter every death." And yet in every firm conviction there is also a not-knowing: "Something becomes whole for me—I don't know what it is."

Third, *in this work of holding-together-the-people-and-God we meet a different kind of power.* There is great power in her assertion that "God is at the bottom of every abyss"—*this* abyss, right now in *this* community's situation. She points to God with courage and she is also wary about her own claiming. She is only the pointer; people must not become dependent on her but "claim their own authority." And so, with passion and openness, this priest finds her power in pointing to that space where God and people meet.

Summary:
Signs of Integrated Authority in the Ministries of Laity and Clergy

We have looked at these stories of clergy and lay ministry with a special focus on the paradoxical and "porous" quality of Integrated authority. Let's examine that sign first, and then look for the other indicators of Integrated authority.

Integrated Authority is Paradoxical.

"Blessed are those who hunger and thirst for righteousness." This seems an appropriate text for summarizing the stories of laity who live with the contradictions posed by the world: recall, for example, Ruth Shinn's decision to support administration positions with which she does not agree because she believes in a two-party system. Or the open spaces that emerge between a rock and a hard place for laity like Peter Sherer who, facing the necessity of firing an employee, agonizingly seeks to uphold his values in a situation where they can be expressed only in fragmentary ways.

"Blessed are the poor in spirit": with this text we might gather up the paradoxical stories of clergy. Dwight Lundgren, who finds his ministry between the call to be an expert and the beckoning toward being a "fool for Christ." Dee Crabtree, who craves integration and harmony but doesn't back away from necessary conflict or from her struggles with the tension between being open to others and affirming her own point of view. Dorothy McMahon, whose sense of her authority arises most powerfully out of her vulnerability, and who holds up brokenness in broken bread in order to witness to life. The clergy in these stories are continually driven into conflict with what they want to embrace unquestioningly and forced to face what they would rather avoid. In refusing to grasp power, these pastors claim their authority. It's as though we give them a place where they can do what we all need them to do: hold up the Integrated vision. The poor in spirit carry out their ministry on behalf of those who hunger and thirst for righteousness out in the world, beyond the clergy's sphere of control.

Each of these people, in his or her own way, finds tension and paradox an opening for God. The way they had it all put together is broken apart and new possibilities are revealed. They learn that they don't want to deny difficulties to protect a false integration, for that would only drain off energy and wall off God. The Coach and the Prophet together thus shape a paradoxical church in which mutual support and challenge keep us all growing—a church with a call, active and moving out; a church under judgment, with self-correction built in.

The breaking-open of paradox makes room for all the other signs of integrated authority revealed in these stories.

Authority belongs to God.

These lay people know that authority does not belong to them, or to the powers that be, or even to the church. These clergy know that, ultimately, authority does not belong to them. All these ministries are obediently open to God. Let's look at some of the ways this opening happens.

Each person knows: "My authority is derivative." "My hands only deliver [the sacraments]," says Dorothy McMahon. "I understand the limits of who I am and what I do," confesses Dwight Lundgren. These clergy are pointers.

Our recognition that we are *not* in control helps us affirm that authority belongs to God. Jim Adams, a competent man, acknowledges his blunders. Smart and powerful laity like Judith McMorland and Keith Mason live out this acknowledgment in their painful struggle to exercise appropriate authority with their children.

Our knowing and our not knowing, held together, point to God. The lay prophets assert that authority is given by God, but they know they can't take it for granted that any particular authority is from God. Dwight Lundgren's awe-filled wondering about God is a roomy place where mystery is welcomed in. Dorothy McMahon admits a caveat for every conviction, and yet she affirms that we can enter every abyss because God is at its depth.

Integrated authority doesn't depend on control.

The people in these stories stretch past the compulsion to control, because control as a life principle contradicts that spacious trust, that roominess for the well being and freedom of others revealed in their stories. Mason knows that "the good of the unit or the child is the point" not "who's in charge." Adams knows that when he supports people in an open way, much energy is unleashed, and much is accomplished, but "it may not be what I had in mind." For these interviewees, "getting it all together" through control is relinquished for a larger integration that embraces other people, the immediate situation, oneself, and God.

When clergy relinquish control, they have a new kind of relationship with laity. Here we find no clergy-lay codependence, with that tight lock between clergy overfunctioning and lay evasion of responsibility, and with the inevitable result of burnout in the pulpit and boredom in the pew. These clergy define their relationship with laity in quite another way. They define their *own* roles. They issue no lofty pronouncements on "what it means to be a Christian doctor." The approach of these interviewees contrasts with some of the pastors I've encountered at "Sharing the Ministry" conferences where it soon became clear that by "sharing ministry" many of them really meant "getting the lay people to do what I want." Instead, for Adams, grace means that "I am able to withhold my attempts at controlling." And for McMahon, "The agenda of our parish is not mine...and I'm always grateful that it isn't."

Hierarchy is not the point.

These clergy and laity aren't locked together in a dominant-subordinant pattern. In these stories we see strong, independent laity who ask for support from the church and protest assertively when that support is not forthcoming. Laity like Ruth Shinn, out planting collaborative practices in a hierarchical system, would have no interest in belonging to a church where "Father knows best." Colin Bradford, affirming his own ministry based on experience rather than formal training, wants a complementary rather than a hierarchical relationship with his religious leader.

These clergy's sense of their own expertise contrasts sharply with the kind of expertise that defines the others as incompetent or dependent. They have succeeded in resisting the seductions of the clergy John Fletcher described, who responded to increasing requests for help by pumping up inflated images of themselves as all-powerful helpers.[3]

Instead we find here collaborative pictures of clergy relationships with laity—like the Coach, who wants laity to be strong and respects their worldly callings. And like the self-awareness of Dorothy McMahon, who knows she, too, sits under the judgment of the "word *we* don't want to hear." These clergy don't treat laity like servants or "amateurs"; instead they follow their Lord in a ministry stance that says, "I have called you friends."

These people experience their authority as integrated.

Lay people forge out an integration in the world. "I'm an experiential Christian," says Colin Bradford. Supported by a church that honors and values his Integrated authority, he pulls his ministry together on the run. Mason presses the church to concern itself with *life* and fights for a vision of Integrated authority that will *include* the church.

The clergy in this study struggle to find an integration within the church that will include the world. Dee Crabtree's ministry is a process of "integrating within me all of what's happening around" so that the initiatives of the minister, the lives of the people, and the openness of all of that to God take on the responsive, fluid character of a dance. Holding the power of the sacraments out before her, Dorothy McMahon comes to her parishioners as "a broken human being who bears witness...to the grace of God...and...how I see that happening in a group of people..." For both Dee and Dorothy, pastoral authority emerges from claiming the power of their own experiences and expecting others to claim the same power.

And so we see clergy dealing with real human concerns and laity incarnating religious concerns in daily life. They approach the enterprise from different directions, but there is in the end no neat separation, but instead a partnership between clergy and laity that leaves both a lot less lonely.

Integrated authority joins the strengths of Received, Autonomous, and Assertive authority.

We see both clergy and laity willing to adopt a *Receiving* posture. In the world lay people have to tough it out, but they look for a chance to be nourished and strengthened in the church for that battle. Clergy, too, can admit they need help, and all (the women most noticeably) are open to receiving from their parishioners. Pastors like these seem able even to receive the help of the laity in their struggle to reject the inappropriate adoration that can fester in ecclesiastical settings.

At the same time, pastors and lay people are *Autonomous*—they find their authority in an authentic centeredness. For Adams, authority means being "real." McMahon traces her journey to the discovery that "integrity has authority beyond anything that we can imagine." Verna Dozier holds up the conviction that free-lance Christians can't look to any institution for their authority. These lay people claim the autonomy to stand back and take enough distance to see the prophetic task.

And then they move *assertively* into action. Mason is "willing to be a nuisance," but his confrontive posture is flexible enough to permit him to ask for support. For all of these leaders assertiveness is no small, purely personal enterprise, but their energy and boldness become an invitation to the whole community.

Integrated leaders evoke the authority of others.

These leaders invite other people's authority by giving four messages.

1. *I am with you.* They start with people where they are. Dwight Lundgren is "happy with where people are at the moment." Dorothy McMahon finds authority in "deeply connecting with the authentic feelings of people." She finds receiving their confidences "a great honor" and "privilege." (How different from the leader whose words and actions give the message "You need fixing" and "I have the fix you need.") These church leaders respect not only individual parishioners but the whole world of laity outside the church's doors.

2. *I am not your authority.* When leaders, while standing supportively at hand, say "I'm *not* the one for you to depend on," they offer an invitation to what looks like emptiness and then provide supportive companionship while people venture into that emptiness on their own. When Dwight Lundgren says, "I won't take over your responsibility," he invites you to consider taking it yourself. When Dee Crabtree says "we're practicing here," she defers to the players' real game, during which their coach will retreat to the sidelines.

3. *We are equals.* We can see many of these leaders positioning themselves alongside their colleagues, as when Ruth Shinn invites the secretary to take a turn chairing the meeting. Collaborative leaders evoke others' authority.

4. *I invite your gifts, your partnership, your authority.* Lundgren uses his exegetical skills not to tell people what the Bible says, but to create an experience to which they may respond: "Oh, *that's* how you do it!" Ruth Shinn tells me with delight that her secretary is learning public speaking. Welcoming many gifts for ministry evokes leaders' gifts, too. When many people are claiming their piece of the action, clergy don't have to do everything, but can do what they're good at. Thus with

satisfaction increased and defensiveness laid to rest, they can more wholeheartedly continue to welcome others' contributions. (I think here of clergy who came to "Sharing the Ministry" conferences suspiciously— "If the lay people do all that, then who will *I* be?"—and left with a new sense of promise.) If church is not the central place, but a useful place, ministry in the church becomes a helpful opportunity to train for ministry in the world, and people move out with heightened confidence.

People with Integrated authority can inhabit a wider world.

Lay people push the boundaries out into the world. Judith McMorland knows that "you can have a dynamic ministry in the classroom just as much as you do in the parish pew." These lay people are a colony of heaven on the move, carrying Integrated values out into a world dominated by Control, while the clergy provide their base camp.

And clergy, too, are explorers. Dorothy McMahon carries the sacraments out to oppressed people in a secular city—Aboriginals, prostitutes, those who live in despair and fear. And every one brackets ecclesiastical preoccupations in favor of standing by the laity looking at the world outside the church's doors.

Write your own story.

How do paradox and open spaces emerge in your own experience of exercising authority? Tell a story about disjunctures: a place where things didn't fit, or where things collided or contradicted each other, or where the false assumptions you didn't know you had were revealed. Or perhaps your story will describe a time when all at once the world around you invited you into a new response? Or when your carefully contrived answer suddenly fell apart? Or perhaps a time when you were revealed as inadequate in some way, but even so you encountered a great "Yes!" Perhaps you will get in touch with your story best in a meditative mode; or perhaps by writing it down; or even by finding somebody you want to tell it to and just seeing what story emerges in the telling.

If you're still wondering what story to tell, try one of these pump-primers.

For clergy. As a pastor, do you see a paradox or an open moment...

—when you stood with someone at one of life's boundaries?
—when you had a way to live in your role that worked, but then came to seem inadequate or untenable?
—in a meeting, when the space between the people crackled with a new energy and surprising possibilities emerged?
—when your error was revealed for all to see, and the anticipated disaster did not occur?
—when you didn't get your way and something better happened?
—when you bit your tongue and somebody "got it" or "took hold" (and never noticed your heroic restraint)?
—when you were ministered to by a parishioner?
—when you popped the bubble of your own perceived importance and saw someone grow a little in the face of your own newly discovered ordinariness?
—when you said clearly "This is the way I see it" in a situation where that was very hard to do?
—when you were able to convey "We may safely enter every death"?
—when the shape of your ministry presented you with a paradox that was lifegiving?

For laity. As a worker, parent, or volunteer, do you see a paradox or an open moment...

—at a time when you "got it" that your authority wasn't the main issue?
—when you had to challenge accepted authorities?
—when it seemed impossible to behave lovingly in your office conflict and you wrestled with that at 3 a.m.?
—when you decided to protest your church's action (or inaction) even if it made you look uncooperative and even rude?
—when you invited people you work with to make some decisions when that was not your organization's practice?
—when you challenged your church to make its program relevant to your dilemmas on the job or with the kids?
—when your principles were seriously compromised by the actions of your organization and you faced the possibility of having to quit?

—*when you decided to claim an authority "the authorities" deny you had?*
—*when you struggled with the necessity of firing someone who really needed the job?*
—*when the false assumptions you didn't know you had were revealed?*

CHAPTER VI

Growing in Authority; Being the Church

As we have been exploring how we might hold authority more faithfully as individuals—male and female, clergy and lay—we kept discovering that Integrated authority is *authority from community and for community*. Mature authority moves us beyond the passivity of the many and the control of the few toward the lively richness of the whole body.

In this final chapter we will pull that community dimension of authority from background to foreground. Still joining the biblical picture and human experience, we will now look at corporate pictures and corporate experiences from which learnings about church systems have been distilled. With the illumination from these two "flashlights," we will now look at what it means to be a *community* that lives according to Integrated authority. How can we become that kind of community?

In our clergy-focused churches, for example, how do we stop "blaming all crashes on pilot error"[1] and assuming that lay people are docile passengers (in spite of all our rhetoric to the contrary)? Are there ways of being the church that will help us, as a total system, to welcome the Integrated authority of every member?

How the Church Lost Its Vision of Integrated Authority

Looking at the picture of Jesus' authority drawn by the early church, we can see that the picture, though it has often become dim, is not erased today. As we listen to the stories of our interviewees—present-day men and women, clergy and laity—we know that picture shines brightly for them.

But for many the picture has faded. In order to discover why that happened, let's go back and look at the story again.

After Jesus' death, the Galilean hillbillies (or the enthusiastic but confused "Godspell" children) who followed him had been left empty-handed. Now, suddenly, those who had nothing left to hold on to found that they were given power and love and hope. The invisible Power of a Spirit that could not be grasped took hold of *them* and filled them with energy and joy.

Patterning themselves on their Lord, early church leaders called forth others' authority. Paul had a strong sense of his own apostolic authority; at the same time he found ways to advise unruly New Testament churches on their problems without taking control. He kept teaching them that ministry belongs to all Christians. *All* the parts of the body are important, and "charisma" means not dazzle but offering my small gift, doing what's needed to build up the whole. (I Cor. 12, Rom. 12) The Johannine community pictured the authority of the disciples, not as a gate barred to all but a few, but as an open door that welcomes all of us who follow. The author of I Peter saw that now *all* are a holy priesthood. (2:5, 9)

But the vision of Integrated authority was fragile from the very beginning. The disciples didn't "get it" very often. And in spite of New Testament leaders' efforts to hold up that fragile vision, the church began to slip back under the heavy fist of Control. By the fourth century, the same ranking and control Jesus strongly protested were again taken for granted.[2]

Why do we always keep slipping back? We seem to have a lot of reasons. We feel more secure relying on human hierarchies than on a Spirit blowing in directions we cannot predict. We feel more comfortable when "people like us" are running the show. "Staying on top of things" seems safer than the open spaciousness of trust. Even if we do want to stay true to the open vision, as time goes by we have an itch to "bottle it," to make sure the dream doesn't slip away, that we can grab hold of it at will. It's easier to do it ourselves than to beckon the uncertain gifts of others. We want guarantees that those others will implement the vision the way we think they should. So we draw up guidelines and concentrate on carrying them out to the letter.

It should not surprise us, therefore, to see the church leaders who wrote the Pastoral Epistles beginning to tighten things up. For example, they retreated from the countercultural partnership between men and women we glimpsed in the gospels and in Paul's ministry and instead sought to keep women under control. (E.g. I Tim. 2:11-12) The vision of authority that grasps us in the moment always seems to evolve over time into a bureaucracy *we* can grasp. In Richard Sennett's succinct summary: "Christ inevitably becomes the Church."[3]

And so now, after two millennia, we are left with a church in which clergy have unmanageable jobs, laity have gifts that are ignored and a "ministry" that is often an empty slogan, and women's insights and initiative are still stifled. The ringing rhetoric of the vision we inherited from those early open moments sounds increasingly hollow when we hold up before it the realities of daily church life. Even though it's painful to admit that the gospels' picture of authority has been largely rejected during centuries of church life, admitting the truth is always the first step toward finding our way again.

If the Church were grounded in Integrated authority, what would it look like?

Metaphors: A Paradoxical Way of Holding Up the Vision

"What language shall I borrow...?" asks an old hymn. We have always spoken most powerfully about our vision for the church by using borrowed language—symbols and metaphors. Metaphors help us voice our deepest truths in a way that is friendly with tension and paradox. We stammer toward a reality we cannot grasp, a truth that grasps *us* while respecting our freedom—and leaving the Mystery free as well. Metaphorical language admits that we can't capture God. And when we speak the language of loving confidence instead of proclaiming our grasp of proven certainties, our words leave room for many people. We lay aside our itch for proof and our craving to be right that carve chasms between those who see it our way and those who are "wrong."

And so as we try to discern how a community might live by Integrated authority, let us borrow three metaphors for the church—a colony of heaven, the Body of Christ, Servanthood. For each, let's ask ourselves, "How might we live like the people of God moving into the future under the banner of that metaphor?"

The Church as a Colony of Heaven—or a Laboratory

The Philippians, probably even prouder of their Roman citizenship because they were colonials far from home, must have appreciated Paul's metaphor. We're not going to live like those around us whose "minds are set on earthly things," he told them, for "our citizenship is in heaven." (Phil. 3:19-20)

Colonists remember home and find ways to live in a new land. Those Philippians remind me of the citizens of Christchurch, New Zealand, who, though thousands of miles from England, cherish the ways of home. A visitor—admiring the spired colleges of the university, strolling by a riverfull of ducks, stopping for afternoon tea in a shop whose window curtains are sprigged with dim, diminutive flowers—has to make an effort to remember that this is not a university town back in England. "The ways of home" have a proud profile in the hearts of the citizens of Christchurch, as they did in Philippi. Colonists engage fully in their life here and now, but at the same time they are always conscious that they are "aliens and exiles" (I Pet. 2:11), "strangers and foreigners" (Heb. 11:13)

Like a "colony," a "laboratory" refers to a reality beyond itself. It's a place "alongside." Many of us who have been around the church for a while are familiar with *training* laboratories. In a human relations lab, for example, we can adopt an experimental, learning approach to our behavior. Being right isn't as important as acknowledging *what is*. In a lab, we can *identify* ways of behaving, *analyze* their effect, and *generalize* so that we can begin to imagine how those behaviors would work in other settings outside the lab where we wouldn't feel as free to experiment. In the same way, the church is a laboratory for living where we are liberated from the bottom-line concerns of the world. Church people are given that gift of liberation so that we can take the church enterprise lightly in the service of what concerns us ultimately.

Discovering Truth Together

Let's examine some of the ways we might seek and build truth together in this church that is a colony of heaven or a lab for learning.

We will acknowledge the complexities of life. Instead of artificially simplifying the situation before us so that we can get on top of it, we will take a cue from the laboratory. We will observe carefully the many and diverse participants and notice their complex and shifting interactions. We stay alert, continually taking in new information, learning all the time, just as colonists live freely and responsively between the dearly remembered ways of home and the daily realities of life in this new-found land. The question "*How* are we living here?" becomes more important than any "answer."

Our Integrated leaders find a wealth of clues for meaning and direction as they bring the complexities of their daily life experience to meet the picture in the gospels. Glenn Farquhar-Nicol spends a half hour in silence every morning, holding up the hurts and irritations that beset an honest pastor and working them through. Glenn's way of beginning his day reminds me of my own morning "put-together" time—logging my experiences in my journal, reading the lessons appointed in the daily lectionary, then sitting in silence. The sparks that strike between yesterday's upset and today's gospel lesson light the way for the day that follows.

We will emphasize process, not just content. We get into trouble when we focus only on content. Verna Dozier now says confidently, "We are not saved by being right." But Verna's message, which contradicts the assumptions of the dominant church culture, has been wrested from decades of living. Less mature church people often get very busy about *who's right* and don't notice how we're living together. When we do that, we inevitably start treating each other in ways that contradict the ideas we're selling. When we're anxiously focused on being right, we try to make others agree. Because propositions present us with only two options—to assent or protest—they easily divide and oppress us.

Family systems experts like Edwin Friedman teach us that families can't resolve their important issues by focusing on content. When I move from "my husband should clean up after himself" to "what's going on between us?" we may move out of stuckness into a new place of love and freedom. When we start attending to process, when we start asking "How are we living together here?" we get freed up from the "matter" with which some are trying to control others. Loving God and our neighbors is about an open and willing way to live—not a proposition I try to get you to buy.

Making sense out of my life—the religious task of "putting it back together"—is a process, not a product. Articulations of our meaning-making will emerge, but they are like bubbles surfacing from the deep waters of life, disolving into the next wave as it rushes to meet us, not to be captured and sold. Each of us needs to discover our own meaning. And so leaders like Jim Adams are kenotic ("I can't hand my answers over to other people"), providing open space for the other's energetic, active meaning-making. Jesus engages the life of his listeners with questions and challenges that hand the enterprise back to them. "The kingdom is *in your midst* or *within you.*" "Come, follow me." *Live* the truth, for people don't really know the truth until they live it together. When our way of living is open to God and our neighbors, it is fluid, evolving, poised on the edge of the future's mystery while at the same time true to the present moment and illuminated by symbols from the tradition we have inherited from the past. The *way we are living* is congruent with the truth we proclaim.

Instead of debating, we can engage in creative, mutual truth-seeking. If we are going to engage in mutual exploration of truth, ac-knowledging its shifting and complex nature, and paying attention to the way we live with each other (not just to selling our version of the truth), we'll come together in a different spirit from that found in many churches. If you sat in as process observer in a typical church gathering, you would notice a pattern like this: one person gets up and holds the floor with a carefully prepared message designed to convince the others, who listen in silence.

Now bring your sharp ears and pen and clipboard to a weekend conference where, at the Sunday eucharist, one participant has suggested that we might collaboratively create a sermon by holding a conversation about the insights that arose during the weekend's work and the lessons we just chose. One woman ventures a half-finished thought, and some-one else adds a fragment of an insight, while another connects it with the gospel lesson. As we build this conversational sermon together, we discover that we have been nurturing not only ideas but ourselves.[4]

I am trying to carry the spirit of this creative, mutual truth-building into conversations in other settings. Instead of carefully preparing My Message, I am trying to come more openly to the other person, wonder-ing where he might be, starting with a question. The response can guide me to ask another question or build on my partner's comment. Loosened up from grasping ego, I can sometimes *name* what needs naming, not earnestly, but lightly—perhaps in a throw-away tease that offers "take it or leave it." I may learn someday to trust enough to follow the advice in Mark 13: "do not worry beforehand about what you are to say, but say whatever is given to you at that time..."

We can broaden such an approach to a congregational setting with Jack Harris's description of a church "in which inner transformation can occur": it's "as though the church said...'We invite you to join us in a journey. Bring who you are, learn what you need to learn that deepens your relationship with people, embrace the unexpected and be open to new sights that may bring you to a place that we do not attempt to specify.'"[5] As creative, mutual truth-seekers, perhaps we may become the "co-workers with the truth" of whom the author of III John spoke.

We will find Integrated rather than Control ways of doing theology. Our active stance as co-authors of our faith releases energy in the whole body! Many of us wake up to the chagrined realization that somehow in seminary we absorbed an attitude of contempt for lay people. When Jean Haldane, while interviewing laity, remarked on the rich faith journeys being recounted, her respondents explained, "Nobody ever asked me about this before!" But when we move beyond condescension and diffident silence, we become energized "co-workers with the truth."

The clergy role is key, say our interviewees, because the clergy are granted access to people's lives and experiences. Out of their common, lived experience, says Dorothy McMahon, "the people have *given* me my sermons." These clergy are not fixers, who study parishioners' experiences for clues about where they need repairs. The pastor as repairman would aim to get people marginally functional again and then quit fixing. But instead of a deficiency mentality, these pastors have their eyes on *abundance*: they aim to evoke the gifts and growth of those who may become saints and leaders far more creative and powerful than their pastor. Those pastors' approach reminds me of Paul's words about "our authority, which the Lord gave for building you up and not for tearing you down..." (II Cor. 10:8.) *Access*, not *status*, is the point of privilege for pastors.

All of us, pastors and the rest of the people, are "co-workers with the truth" that transforms our lives when the depths of our experience—our yearnings, our shaky places, our deepest joys, fears, and failures—connect with the symbols and stories of our tradition. Meaning-coming-alive is an open, collaborative process in which all of us, and all dimensions of me, participate—just as Martha and Jesus pressed deep into an experience of anguished loss and moved quickly past a tired recital of doctrine toward a graced encounter from which these words burst forth: "*I am* the resurrection and the life" and "Yes, Lord, I believe."   Two joined mind and heart in a radiant moment of knowledge through love.

If truth sparks forth from an energy-filled meeting of experience and symbol, "experts" expounding on "the truth" is an ill-fitting method. Instead leaders can speak from their own wrestling and discoveries in a way that invites, "Now let's hear from you"; and the preacher's exegesis can evoke the response, "Oh, *that's* how you do it!"

This energizing search, embracing all of me and all of us, will include "prizing the emotional side of parish life," as Jack Harris pointed out—"tenderness, closeness, fighting, hurt, talking through, forgiving, deepened understanding—all the emotional raw material that everywhere constitutes the joy and pain of human life."[6] The cost of ignoring this side of parish life is superficiality, boredom, and walled-off fear. The promise of prizing it is reality, liveliness, and growth in ministry.

At its best, the experience of "church" is set up to enhance the possibility that people will experience those transforming moments when love and truth flash together. When my life has been changed, I love those people! We have been through despair and joy together, and, like Mary and the beloved disciple at the foot of the cross, we suddenly know: "This is my family." Our discovery creates community ("these are the people who were with me in that astounding moment"), and our memories are sustained by community ("remember the time when...?").

And so we return to our corporate starting point. Our exploration of Integrated authority, which we first pursued from within, from the viewpoint of the individual person's experience, here moves back toward community, toward the corporate vision that undergirds all Integrated authority, toward the colonists' memory and hope of home.

One Body, Many Members, Many Gifts: The Church as System

A second metaphor for the church that can point the way toward living corporately with Integrated authority is *the Body of Christ.*

How Body/Systems Thinking Helps Us

In *The Equipping Pastor,* Stevens and Collins show how Paul's metaphor of the Body of Christ and the contemporary understanding of an organization as a system come together.[7] I see three major ways in which borrowing those two kinds of language points the way to a church that lives by Integrated authority.

First, *the contradiction between diversity and unity is overcome.*
"Now there are varieties of gifts,   *but the same Spirit; and*
there are varieties of services,   *but the same Lord,*
and there are varieties of activities,

                                          but it is the same God who
                                          activates all of them in
                                          everyone.
To each is given
the manifestation of the Spirit   *for the common good."*
                                          (I Cor.12:4f)

The gifts of the Spirit aren't given so that we can set ourselves up over or against different people with other gifts. Instead each of us has a unique contribution to make toward building up the one body in which we all find our truest identity.

Paul emphasizes the common purpose of the many gifts by holding up, above them all, the one gift that joins us together freely and joyfully: love. Leaders who understand systems theory can follow Paul's advice about placing love above all the valuable individual gifts in very practical ways. Suppose Joe comes to you to complain about Everett, and then Everett confides to you that Joe has undercut his leadership. Instead of siding with either Everett or Joe, you can *side with the relationship between them* and encourage them to talk with each other—even, if they are reluctant, offering to go with one to speak with the other, in order to work out the problem.

The basic unit of the body/system is the whole. But diversity doesn't endanger the whole—it enhances and enriches the whole. If we are diverse because God's generous grace showers us with gifts, then I can't say "I don't count," because *I am part of that richness*. And you can't say you don't need what I have to offer, because this rich oneness *does* need what I can give. "On the contrary," says Paul, "the members of the Body that seem to be weaker are indispensable." (Rom. 12:24) Having "gifts that differ," let's *use* them, instead of one member putting down another's contribution or taking over a job someone else is better suited to carry out.

Body/systems language helps, second, by affirming that *the parts are interdependent.*

"For as in one body we have many members, and not all the members have the same function, so we, who are many, are one body in Christ, and individually we are members one of another." (Rom 12:4-5) You all depend on me to exercise my gift, and I depend on all of you. This means that "If one member suffers, all suffer together with it; if one member is honored, all rejoice together with it." (I Cor. 12:26)

Since all the components of a system are interdependent, a change in one part will cause changes in other parts. None of us has much power to change anybody but ourselves. But, just as in your family a change in one member's behavior shifts the other members' roles and relationships, if you, a lay leader in your congregation, grow into Integrated authority, you will make a difference to other members.

The interdependent complexity of a system can help us understand why it is so hard to change it. Because change in one part of the system requires adjustment in every other part, the process will take time and we will need a strategy that arises from our clarity about where our whole church is headed.

The third pointer toward a church that lives by Integrated authority is this: *the body and the system reach beyond themselves.*

Not only are all the parts of the system interrelated, the system is connected to the larger world that surrounds it. We keep learning about the mutual interrelationship between families or congregations and the neighborhood and culture in which they live. These relationships of mutual influence reach not only through space but through time. Patterns repeat themselves "from generation to generation." My friend who divorced when her daughter was five and always seemed to be embattled with her mother has been struggling with *her* daughter, whose marriage ended when *her* daughter was five. In the church whose pastor's sexual misconduct is tearing up the congregation, we may well find the halls decked with portraits of former clergy whose sexual exploits have long been shrouded secrets, whispered by previous generations.[8]

The transcendent referrents of the body of Christ seem also to extend beyond space and time. Human relationships signify great mysteries, saw the writer of Ephesians, as he pointed to mysterious correspondences glimpsed in the love of husband and wife: "this is a great mystery and I am applying it to Christ and the church." (Eph. 5:32)[9] The church as body of Christ exists to present Christ, in all his fullness, to the world. Thus the body/system includes phenomena we can capture in genograms—but also stretches toward connections over which the mind cannot assert its grasp but toward which faithful hearts can reach with wondering trust.

What good will it do us, then, to link systems theory and the metaphor of the Body of Christ in this way? Stevens and Collins point to a number of ways we can use this conjunction of concepts. It gives us a way to look at the church as a whole while acknowledging its complexities. It encourages us to appreciate the rich diversity of the members' gifts. An awareness of the body/system helps us move toward humility and trust—and even playfulness. It opens out our vision to include not only the world beyond the church but also mysterious connections that transcend the reach of our linear minds.

So how might we live differently in the power of that symbol—"Body of Christ"—enfleshed in a practical understanding of how human systems work? What would we *do*?

Most importantly, *we can look at "leadership" and "membership" in a new way*. The old way put the leaders on top and the members on the bottom. When we assume we have to stay in control and keep the subordinants in line, we do things like this:

—We *don't* evoke their gifts because then they will be harder to control. (Instead we keep lay people busy washing the altar linens and seeing to repaving the parking lot.)

—We *don't* allow out-of-control spaces. (If we keep people busy following the regulations, they won't use their energy in creative ways that might make mischief for the people in control.)

But in the Body, leadership and membership have a different

relationship. Humility and initiative join hands. If I know I don't "have it all," I will want to bring others' rich potentialities to birth. We will balance two kinds of activities: discernment, which welcomes diverse talents and ideas, and ordering or coordinating, which bring all that wealth of gifts together into a coherent whole.

In the church we have had a lot more experience with ordering than with *evoking people's diverse gifts*. So let's focus now on that neglected task of leadership.

How do we go about evoking gifts?

1. Expect energy for ministry from ordinary people.

We'd rather look for an extraordinary leader who is going to swoop down and make it all right for us. We are all agog about "charismatic" authority, which is considered mysterious and sought in celebrities. Are we projecting our own neglected gifts on these objects of our obsessive attention? In a congregation, we fall in love with the new pastor—but the honeymoon is short. All the contributions that we and our fellow parishioners might make look insignificant next to our newly revived hope that we have found the "whole loaf" that will, at last, fill us as we long to be filled.

But among these candidates at whom we gaze so eagerly, no whole loaf is to be found. In our search for "big deals" we find instead inflated hopes, punctured balloons, and painful crashes. Wearying of that se- quence, we may discover to our delight that God yearns to give us the whole loaf, and that God is giving us to each other, so that we can re- ceive from each other the little pieces of bread that we are in fact able to offer one another. And it is enough.

Glenn Farquhar-Nicol sees the congregation's authority as residing in the gifts offered by all the members of the community, and he keeps holding up that vision in the face of constant efforts by parishioners to turn him into the "big deal" leader! We saw this same theme in Samuel's leadership. The people kept pestering him: "Give us a king to govern us!" When Samuel's irritation burst out in his prayer, the Lord assured Samuel that he was not alone in his displeasure: "Just as they have done to me, from the day I brought them up out of Egypt to this day, forsaking

me and serving other gods, so also they are doing to you." (I Sam. 8:8)
Holding up the same motif of authority found in the gifts of the community, Stevens and Collins call us to focus on *leadership, not leaders,* and
to work toward *the widest possible release* of leadership.

2. Open up authority to everybody.

In the New Testament, we kept seeing a picture of authority as accessible: it is continually being *given* by the Father to the Son, by Jesus to
the disciples—who often look more like stumblebums than superleaders,
but who are nevertheless models of all Christians.

Jesus called those disciples "friends, not servants," "because I have
made known to you everything that I have heard from my Father." (Jn.
15:15) This is the opposite of the expert ("I know and you don't.") This
friendly openness we see in one who was criticized for dining with tax
collectors and prostitutes is reminiscent of divine Wisdom, the hostess
who, having set her table, calls "Turn in here!" "Come, eat of my bread
and drink of the wine I have mixed." (Prov. 9:4-5) The picture of
ourselves as friends and guests contradicts the idea of "lower down."
"Higher up" or "lower down" is just not what it's all about. And anyhow, the gospels turn everything topsy-turvy: what was down is up, and
what was up is down.

"Apostle," meaning "one who is sent out," is less important as a
title than as information about what those leaders *do.* That's true of our
interviewees, who see their authority not as a matter of hierarchy but as a
matter of function. They, too, are messengers. The image of delivery
boys effectively contradicts the idea of "higher up."

This open picture challenges many common understandings of
authority in our churches. The biblical picture is not a closed down,
protective picture but a broad one, reaching out hospitably to a world
that keeps getting wider.

Instead, this open picture of authority holds exciting implications
for leadership in our churches. Leaders with Integrated authority will
want to locate authority in the whole body. This open authority contrasts
with the view of those who justify autocratic methods on the grounds that
"we are dealing with ultimate truth here." That's exactly the point: if
truth is ultimate, we *don't* own it. This perspective may point a way for
nonauthoritarian churches to claim their authority clearly. We *don't* give

up power when we give up control—instead, we gather more power by releasing the gifts of many people. Leaders of open, nonauthoritarian churches are like community organizers, *evoking a whole community of authority*.

3. Encourage self-differentiation.

As one grows in love of God and an experience of oneness with God, paradoxically one grows also toward being more distinctively oneself. (Sometimes this distinctiveness has been symbolized by the taking on of a new *name*, as when Jacob becomes Israel or Simon becomes Peter. Many of my women friends, growing into all they're meant to be, leave behind childish or diminishing nicknames and claim the name given to them in baptism.) Our experience with God flows out into our experience with each other in the body of Christ, helping us find new ways to live out the paradox of oneness and distinctiveness.

Without this paradoxical grace, the church finds it difficult to embrace both unity and diversity—to know that unity does not mean sameness and that diversity does not mean independence. Seeking to preserve themselves, institutions emphasize unity at the cost of diversity. When conflict threatens, we fear our unity will splinter, so we clutch at it ("We all think the same here.")

Institutions that tend toward the Control/authoritarian end of the spectrum and those that are passive and "nice" both stress unity at the cost of diversity. Control institutions often assert the leader's individuality and assertiveness at the cost of others' potential contributions. The charismatic leader dazzles the followers, encouraging their projections and weakening their confidence in their own as-yet-unevoked gifts. The group tries to find oneness in the authoritarian or charismatic leader, rather than claiming its unity and diversity in God.

Passive institutions grasp for unity by fuzzing up differences in a cloud of nervous niceness. People are afraid that acknowledging differences will put their togetherness at risk. The "nice" leader surrenders the opportunity to offer his or her own unique contributions and becomes indistinguishable from the group, confirming others' fears that autonomy and assertiveness are too risky. And so here, too, the members fuse under the banner of group unity rather than claiming their unity and diversity in God.[10]

In contrast, those who seek discernment and try for consensus when that is possible are trying to live in the tension. They are willing to invest time and effort in seeing to it that factions do not do violence to one another. At the same time they seek to realize the richness of the whole body, in which the parts take on new shape as they find ways to work together.

Unity does not mean sameness; diversity does not mean individualism. We need to find ways to live out that insight in our own lives and in the church at large. We can encourage each other to live in the tension between the authority of each individual and our responsibility and blessedness as a member of the Body, for we can enjoy both. By grace, what a man often approvingly names "self-definition" and what a woman often thinks of as "paying more attention to *being* than *doing*" emerge as two faces of the same reality. *Be who you are.* And all doings will flow from that. As I grow in trust, I will have less need to grasp a one-sided certainty either in self-protective distancing or in gluing myself anxiously to you. As my "I am" is increasingly defined in God, my doings will flow more and more from love and truth. I will be who I am; you will be who you are; and we will become trusting enough to allow and even cherish the space between us in which graceful encounters may happen. In words from Rumi: "Out beyond ideas of wrongdoing and right doing, there is a field. I'll meet you there."[11]

As I seek to live in this graced paradox, I will be helped by moving back and forth between retreat and involvement. I need times like Jesus' lonely nights on the hills spent in communion with the Father, to let my being become truer and to discern the doings that may spring from that inner truthfulness. And then, taking my cue from Jesus' return to teaching and healing among the crowds, I can move out into my daily work and relationships to engage usefully with others and to receive support.

As in our individual and congregational lives, the Church at large stands in need of defining itself and taking authority for its own life. Main line churches, rather than subordinating their special truth to the discipline of the human sciences or defining themselves in anxious or contemptuous reaction to evangelicals, can take authority to claim their own unique religious perspective. The present pressure of diminishing numbers, resources, and cultural clout experienced by mainstream bodies *could* encourage self-definition, as the catacombs did for our forebears. People who are not swollen by Control and dulled by arrogance have a better sense of who they are, experience a healthier unity, and allow more freedom for diversity. In their prosperous heyday, when "everybody knew who we were," mainline churches could take their identity for granted. As white males have been discovering, "our" values were as pervasive as the air we breathe and as hard to define. Now our authentic being has often shrunk into a preoccupation with busy doings, and our corporate bonds are weak and infected with fear. In our new and shaky minority status, we will have to seek our true unity not only within but beyond the circle of "people like us," to define our being, not just in timid nostalgia for the old homogeneous club, but as an open vision for the future.

4. Allow space in which gifts may be evoked and many members' Autonomy and Assertiveness can be welcomed.

God shrinks. Jesus empties himself. As Adams concluded, "the disciples discovered their own authority...by Jesus refusing to be the answer for them." You have to relinquish control in order to welcome the gifts and initiative of others. When Dee Crabtree and her colleagues deftly created in the center of Colchester church a space that welcomed the authority of lay ministers in the world, that authority gathered new energy, not only within the congregation but in offices, factories, homes, and community organizations. Roman Catholic communities in Latin America, suffering a shortage of priests, discovered that ordinary members were not just consumers: laity became leaders. Allowing space has very practical implications in small Protestant churches, too. Churches often stay small because their clergy want to hang onto authority. Congregations cannot grow to Program size (150-350 active members)[12] unless the pastor is willing to relinquish control and share authority with laity.

Because allowing space is so crucial to welcoming authority in the whole body, I want now to develop in some detail some space-making strategies.

Recognizing That Authority Roles Are Temporary:
A Practical Way to Allow Space in Which the Authority
of the Whole Body May Be Evoked

Leaders in church and society so commonly strive to hold on to their
authority roles that it's easy to assume that these roles *are* permanent.
But if we look at our interviewees' view of their authority, at our primary
human experience in healthy families, and at the way Jesus and Paul held
their authority, we see a different picture: an acceptance of the temporary nature of all authority roles. This way of holding one's authority as
leader as though it were "on loan" is a way of living out that the Body is
one, with many members, and many gifts.

Some of our interviewees gave compelling testimonies to the way
temporary authority roles can honor and encourage the gifts of all the
members. Ruth Shinn is delighted to see ordained leaders at First
Congregational Church sitting in the front pew along with lay liturgists
on Sunday morning: "When it's their time they step forward and then
they return to the pews; and so we are all together worshipping God...
They *take their turn*, and I think it's a powerful symbol." Judith
McMorland's eyes were opened during a sabbatical: she found the
opportunity to step out of her usual authority role and be a follower an
occasion of important learnings. "There are not many situations where
I'm ever a follower, and that's not good for me...that's an underdevel-
oped part of me. [I'd like to] see much greater flexibility in people's
roles, *so that they weren't permanently anything*, but could experience
being a priest in a parish, and could then experience *not* being." In all
these positive experiences with leadership "on loan," there's an Integrated sitting-loose to power, a trust that there is enough authority in the
body to go around.

When families are working well, mothers and fathers expect to
loosen and finally relinquish their roles as authority figures. The mother's
task keeps shifting as the children grow. In their study of mothers,
Belenky et al. found that "the inequality between parent and child was
only temporary." As they grew up the daughters found a new relationship with their mothers that included *equality* (instead of a one-up/one-
down relationship), *collegiality* ("Now we do it together"), *intimacy*
("We can both move out vulnerably into the space between us"), and
trust ("We can give ourselves confidently to this partnership"). These

mothers' openness to the moment's requirement and their willingness to discern what needs doing right now stand in contrast to authority based on control. Their embracing of functional authority in the service of the other is a profound way of living out "Authority belongs to God."

Fathers, too, stand ready to relinquish their authority roles, says Richard Sennett. "No one is strong forever; parents die, children take their place...authority is not a state of being but an event in time governed by the rhythm of growing and dying."[13] Paternalism distorts that truth of fatherhood: "The master is blinded by his own power; the pleasure of domination makes him too insensitive to recognize that it must come to an end."[14] "The children of Pullman and Stalin are never expected to grow up..."[15] We wisely look to our private experiences of authority for an understanding that is more complex and more ethical than our public institutions will allow.

This true authority imaged in a Parent that we learn in life's deepest lessons shines forth in the gospels' picture. We see Jesus in a painful struggle with his own temporariness, a struggle in which he obediently accepts his end, setting the stage for resurrection. You can't go away! protests Peter. "Get behind me, Satan," comes the quick reply. Contradicting his disciples' assumption, Jesus tells them: "it is to your advantage that I go away."(John 16:7) Here is empowering authority as "an event in time"—making space, requiring trust, calling for relinquishment of an attachment that is inappropriate for this moment ("Don't hold me now"). Mary's, and all the disciples', hopes for an authority figure thay can hang on to find ancient echos in Samuel's followers who persisted: "but we are determined." (I Sam. 8:19) Give us a king! A vulnerable messiah, dying, lost to his friends, consistently calls on people to give up the illusion that they could hang on to a permanent authority figure who will fix it for them. As a wise friend of mine puts it, "You can have what you let go of" (hinting again at our recurrent symbol of open, empty hands).

Our mothers and fathers, and the One who patterned his life on his Father, all point to authority roles as temporary, "on loan." This foundational curriculum teaches all of us who borrow those authority roles and all of us who look to authority figures as leaders and guides that we cannot expect our hunger for the eternally dependable to be assuaged by finite authority figures. We cannot own the Eternal, either by grasping control as leaders or by seeking to control our destiny by making our leaders "the answer." We are owned by the Eternal, and all our authority is delegated, derivative, and fragmentary. When we acknowledge that we are fragile people, all of us playing our many small parts, we finally give up looking for a trick to turn what is in essence temporary into something we can have forever.

How the Church Can Embody Temporary Authority

In the Church, as in our families and in the gospel story, authority is exercised by people who come and go. We can live out our awareness that all authority belongs to God, and that it is given to the whole body, by willingly moving in and out of authority roles in our congregations. We can take as our model the itinerant ministry of Paul, whose farewells and letters from distant places brought authority without control to the churches in his care. In our church systems, too, we can find many specific ways to replace the illusion of permanence and control with a willing acknowledgment "that authority is not a state of being but an event in time."

Ordained leaders can fully accept that every pastor is an interim pastor.[16] Just as we can manage not to know, at an existential level, that we are going to die, clergy (except, perhaps, United Methodists) can defend themselves against really knowing that, just as there was a time before they came to this pastorate, there will be a time after they have left. The denial of laity, too, surfaces in anxiety, often intense, when the pastor announces a plan to depart and in the evanescent euphoria commonly experienced during the new pastor's "honeymoon" period. For everyone, the search process provides a crucial and strategic moment of truth. Our congregation learns that the authority for managing our own corporate life is not a rare and extraordinary commodity enshrined in one person, but belongs finally to ordinary people: us. We can renew this awareness through periodic clergy sabbaticals.

Clergywomen tend to bring a more fluid set of assumptions to ordained ministry because they have at best a fragile grasp on any position in the power structure. Because women's positions have been more tentative, and because within them they seem freer to ask for help, a role has not been seen as definer or validator, but functional, and therefore more easily accepted as "an event in time."

Church leaders, ordained or lay, already have at hand a number of practical ways to acknowledge authority roles as temporary. Lay leaders commonly rotate off boards and committees, making room for new people with new gifts. Team leadership, in which two or more take turns "up front," models and encourages moving in and out of role. Some of our interviewees found ways to use their authority strategically, intentionally withdrawing it as feasible. Jim Adams accepted that you have to put up with being an authority figure for starters; Peter Sherer recognized, too, that he could use that role at one stage and give it away at the next. Both displayed a sophisticated acceptance of people's need to work through their issues with authority figures before claiming their own, moving from Received to Autonomous authority and on from there.

Church leaders acknowledge their authority roles as temporary in parts of the church system beyond the congregation, as well. United Methodist District Superintendents commonly return to parish ministry after a stint as executive. Conversations with ELCA bishops, who are elected, not for life, but for a term, have convinced me that they hold their authority "on loan" more than bishops in other traditions. Moving between parish and judicatory roles should provide exciting opportunities to carry learnings between local church and wider church, to apply their awareness of the possibilities and problems in one kind of ministry to the wise conduct of the other. Church consultants are the acknowledged "temporary ministers" par excellence, entering church systems as coaches in problem solving and then leaving local leaders to solidify and implement their new learnings on their own.

These are all ways of living out our awareness that we don't need titles to prove we're okay; that's already accomplished. We can hold our authority as *given* in order to do what needs doing, rather than grasping it to feed our ego and power needs. Thus we live out our knowledge that authority is given to the *church*, and when we relinquish our roles after a time, we elicit and affirm the authority of rising new leaders.

Roles *will* be relinquished, in any event. If we move beyond denial and look with open eyes at the inevitable transfer of authority, we will see new opportunities for building up the confidence and competence of the whole body. In so doing, we acknowledge that all human adventures in authority are fragmentary and finite, and we hold ourselves open to the transcendent authority to which they point.

The Church as Servant: Doing What's Needed

"I am among you as one who serves." (Luke 22:27)

A primary New Testament metaphor for the church and its leadership is
that of *servant*. Most of us spend quite a lot of energy trying to get to be
the boss and trying to get *out* of the role of underling. This certainly was
true for the disciples who, on the way, walking behind Jesus, "argued
with one another who was the greatest." (Mark 9:34) But they must have
suspected that this preoccupation was not in line with their leader's picture of authority because when he asked them what they had been dis-
cussing, "they were silent." No, he explains patiently one more time,
"Whoever wants to be first must be last of all and servant of all." (9:35)
Again he tells them that the Son of man "came not to be served but to
serve..." (10:45) Jesus' message counters our lust for superiority from a
paradoxical angle: being "greater" *really* means being a servant.

Jesus makes it crystal clear that he intends his servant role to be a
model for the disciples' behavior. As he finishes washing their feet, he
translates action into direction: "I have set you an example." (Jn. 13:15).
"You also ought to wash one another's feet." (vs. 14)

But Jesus is not only the model for action; we are also to look for
him in those who teach us what needs doing—the poor, the hungry, the
powerless. "Just as you did it to one of the least of these...you did it to
me." (Mt. 25:40) Captured by the vision of Servant Leadership, Robert
Greenleaf emphasizes "doing to the least": all our actions are to be
tested by the question, "Will it benefit the least powerful?"

And so as servant and served, Christ is to be truly all in all. Do as I
did, for I am your example. And when you have done as I did, "you did
it to me." If Jesus is the model, *and also* to be discerned in the object of
service, the up/down perspective to which we obsessively cling has been
effectively contradicted.

Even if we try to translate our dominant/subordinant perspective
into something a little more subtle and envision ourselves, not quite as
rulers, but as competent experts who will fix things up for those who
need fixing, we do not get the go-ahead from this picture of Jesus in the
gospels. They keep saying to him, "When are you going to fix it?" They
shout it to him on the cross: *"Now* fix it." But the enraged taunts are
directed at one who has surrendered power, who will not take control.

Unlike those who seek to be honored for their expertise, Jesus is found *in* the "least" when we serve them. He doesn't take over; he honors them. He seeks a reciprocal relationship. "What do you want me to do for you?" "Go: *your faith has made you well*." (Mk. 10:52) So even the more sophisticated versions of our cherished dominant/subordinate arrangements fall away when we look at that gospel picture. God always treats me with respect, even with *honor*, and with great care for my freedom.

I see an extra hint about how freedom and service might fit together in Paul's admonishment: "through love become slaves to one another." (Gal. 5:13) Love does turn "service" into utter freedom! Doing something for my beloved feels like playtime—there's nothing I'd rather be doing. Here again, up/down control arrangements spin off into irrelevancy.

The author of I Peter adds one more piece to the puzzle: "Serve one another with whatever gift each of you has received." (4:10) *And so, through grace everything is provided*: the model for serving, the one to serve, the power of love, and the gifts we need in order to do what the situation requires of us.

"I am among you as one who serves." That simple statement says being a servant means *not centering in the ego* but *doing what's needed*. As long as I am grasped by the superior/inferior preoccupation, I can't pay attention to the thing most needful. But the servant metaphor offers me a life-giving alternative: finding my example in Jesus, finding Jesus in the one who needs service, experiencing the joy and freedom that can come from being servants to one another through love, and finding that I have what it takes to do what's needed.

"I have set you an example": servanthood as a pattern for the church

Chosen, serving in suffering and blessedness, mysteriously pointing-beyond—the "form of a Servant," that mysterious metaphor from the Hebrew Scriptures, helped the early church's "fellow servants" find meaning in Jesus' life and in their own lives. Like other metaphors for the church, "Servant" calls the church to reach beyond itself toward God and to the world.

Ministry in the church is a servant to ministry in the world, as many

of our interviewees, clergy and lay, told us in the last chapter. The
"minister" is not the rector/ruler or expert repairman but the servant of
that ministry, called to "serve God, and people, without any thought of
personal acclaim and/or public recognition."[17] Clergy and lay leaders in
the church have been telling us how they work to make the church's
service to the world real. They use in-church ministries as a training
ground for ministry in families, factories, and fields. They help people
become wiser and stronger as they "oscillate" between church service
and worldly service, reflecting on the challenges out there as they help
each other discover skills for facing daily tests. Servant leaders in the
church develop collaborative styles that empower fellow servants among
the laity, so that our *way* of working serves the task to which we are
called. The leaders at Colchester Church notice that the church needs to
be organized differently, so that it really does say "go out into the world"
not "come and rest in the church." Leaders in other churches make the
best of present structures for the time being, but hold fast to the key
principle: seeing ministries *inside* the church as a laboratory for learning
how to do what's needed *outside* the church.

The Servant Leader: Beyond Control and Passivity

Servant leaders are neither controlling nor passive, but active, responsible, working collaboratively with their fellow servants to do what's
needed.

They strike out beyond the stuck-together symbiosis between controlling leader and passive follower, which adds up to "nice." If I lead
and you follow, there will be no conflict, and our relationship will be
neat and symmetrical, but lifeless. A system in which the "strong" call
the shots and the "weak" do what they're told is controlled, static, and
predictable. If we venture beyond control and passivity we will discover
instead multiplicity, contrapuntal richness, liveliness, and tension.

Servants also move beyond another way we commonly split reality:
reactive "rubberbanding" from enchantment with one simple answer to
its opposite. When "empowerment" didn't save us, for example, we
lunged back toward authoritarianism. Grabbing one pole of any of life's
tensions ends by discrediting that simplistic answer; we have to admit
that it simply won't work. Fleeing to the opposite pole in our disappoint-
ment, we will inevitably find that, too, a partial truth, a failed savior—the

inevitable result when people try "to capture the vision instead of allow-ing the vision to capture them."[18]

A way to stay in the tension is indicated by Paul's paradoxical statement to the Corinthians that Christ "is not weak in you, but is powerful in you. For he was crucified in weakness, but lives by the power of God. For we are weak in him, but in dealing with you we will live with him by the power of God... For we rejoice when we are weak and you are strong." (II Cor. 13:3b, 4, 9) Here weakness and strength have a paradoxical, dynamic relationship that explodes with life and surprising possibilities. Paul is not stuck either in playing basket carrier to the Corinthians' basket case or in reacting against the previous de-cade's leadership slogan. As he tries to discern what is needed for building up God's people at Corinth, Paul knows he has many options. He can decide to be gentle and tender when that's what is needed, or he may decide it's time to be strong and severe. Here is no namby-pamby leader; Paul won't hesitate to exert forceful leadership if the situation requires it.

Practically speaking, how would we follow Paul in living out the servant leader paradox? Integrated leaders like Paul, with a posture of openness to the other, might change their leadership design in respon-siveness to the needs of the Corinthians (or the members of your church). They exhibit the courage to stand firm when people's resistance impels them to turn on the leader. Integrated leaders do not major in giving orders or mushy "group-think" passivity. Like Dorothy McMahon, they find alternatives both to absorbing people's pain like a sponge and to solving their problems for them. Integrated leaders like Glenn Farquhar-Nicol say, "I refuse to take that responsibility from them. It's a middle ground—not 'I'll decide for you' or 'You go away and decide.'" Instead these leaders define themselves and find ways to evoke the full maturity of the other—witness Peter Sherer's strategy, both Receptive and Asser-tive, in "taking my step forward in support of whoever took the first step."

Churches with Integrated authority aren't interested in passivity. They reach beyond "niceness," a state of fuzzy illusion that is also a orm of control ("I will be careful to keep everything comfortable because I'm terrified of the alternative"). Those frightened congregations might turn more often to some of the not-so-nice Bible stories like the story of Jesus pushing over the money-changers' tables. Churches founded on

Integrated authority are willing to be called to account, willing to go for excellence instead of just trying to stay out of trouble. These churches follow Paul in their willingness to engage in hard encounters when that's what is needed, and to get the training in conflict management that helps them hang in there through the tough spots. Not content with just being comfortable extensions of the nice living rooms of people like us, these churches reach beyond the private sphere to the world where differences encounter *us*.

Nor are churches with Integrated authority interested in control. Congregations have let go control when they expand their vision beyond the menu of people's problems (that they could fix) to celebrate also the grace in life beyond the church doors—marriages, births, triumphs of justice in the workplace. The church lets go control when it gives up a rigid power system locked in place by the dominants' grasp of power and the subordinants' covetous capitulation, and instead listens for God's new call in the moment and watches for the gifts of many people to follow that call. The church lets go control when clergy and laity, sharing the authority, allow their open partnership to become transparent for God's authority.

The church also relinquishes control by honoring people's need for structural connection in their work without assuming that those must be structures of control. We do need people to whom it matters what we do. We need accountability. We do not necessarily need people to tell us what to do. The church, as a voluntary servant organization released from the world's bottom lines, can explore new ways of making decisions and working together. Look at how Speed Leas and George Parsons guided a large Presbyterian church's staff toward specific ways to live in the tension:

> We recommended that the staff consider differentiating among the types of decisions made and establishing criteria for choosing when decisions would be made by consensus, when they would be made by the person responsible for the work, and when there would be consultation with the senior pastor who would make the final decision. By consensus (that is, through the use of dispersed authority) the staff team called for consensus decision making on certain issues (1) that affected the whole staff; (2) on which there needed to be high commitment, (3) on which there needed to be

significant input from all parts of the organization. Unless there was substantial conflict within the staff on the issue and, after several serious attempts to work the conflict through, the staff was unable to arrive at consensus, the senior pastor would not be the final authority on issues such as establishing the goals of the staff team, agreeing on the staff's corporate prayer and worship life, and determining which decisons are collaborative and which are hierarchical![19]

Let's take a look at how the wider Church might move beyond passivity and control. Main line churches are being pressed toward uncharted frontiers as their old recipes for success fail to cook up any solutions for today's drops in membership and revenue. Christendom has been split between liberals who have tended to accommodate themselves to the culture's agenda and evangelicals who have tended to claim triumphal certainties that work better in private than public life. As churches try to live faithfully in the tension between attending to *what is* and pursuing the transcendent call, they avoid passivity and control when they adhere to the church's own special truth found in the intersection between the symbol that points beyond and our life as we experience it in this moment. Leaving behind accommodation and triumphalism, we can seek instead to find our self-definition in God, stay in touch with real life, and be faithful servants to the world in its dilemmas. Such a church speaks with authority that is both clear and relevant.

The wider Church also moves beyond passivity and control when it stays clearly focused on the *congregation* as the front line for the servant church. Our persistent tendency to be diverted into preoccupations about "who is greater?" often translates into the mistaken assumption that academia or bureaucracy is the place where ministry *really* happens. Even though the status of professors and bishops seems more and more marginal in these days of sea change, it's an attractive commodity to try to hang onto. Those who minister in congregations often feel diffident, second rate. The clergy career ladder encourages the assumption that parish pastors who are "really on the ball" will get promoted to the ranks of the executives or seminary professors, who then may look down on the parish clergy who "can't quite make it" as movers and shakers or who seem biblically unsophisticated. (The bureaucrats and professors generally don't look any further "down the ladder" than the clergy, perhaps taking it for granted that laity, not having "made it to rung one," aren't in the game. And of course they are right.)

Those in seminaries and judicatory offices sometimes lose touch. The bureaucracy has often lost touch with the experiences of laity and ordinary clergy and also with the Bible and the tradition, other than those aspects relating to governance. Seminaries are supposed to be the servants of the church, but somehow "servant" has a way of creeping over toward "intellectual elite." When academic institutions lose their connection with the experience of people and congregations, graduates conclude that their seminary education didn't prepare them for the real tests of parish ministry.

Who will be the greatest? The one who serves ordinary people. Those at the pinnacle of the church hierarchy have often been called "servants of the servants of God." Right on! But how easily and deviously this "servanthood" undergoes an Orwellian mutation into the hierarchical control and ranking that no longer aim just to do what's needed.

In church systems, it is *congregations* that serve ordinary people. Because local churches are on the front lines, worshipping God, trying to do what's useful for the people who come, they are pressed toward noticing what's actually needed and away from the attempt to "lord it over" any other parts of the church. When all of us can say "no" to the Control culture mentality and "yes" to service, when seminaries and judicatories carry out their ministries as servants of the ministries of local churches set in communities, the whole Church is a true follower of One who said "I am among you as one who serves."

Building Integrated Servant Leadership for the Church

What kind of leaders do we need? We may get some support in our search for a nonhierarchical, functional view of leadership by looking at Paul's list of all the things that need doing in the church. He begins Romans 12 by reminding his readers not to "be conformed to this world" and "not to think of yourself more highly that you ought to think, but to think with sober judgment." We are "members one of another." We have been given "gifts that differ." Then Paul lists some of the things that need to be done and what we have been given to do them: "prophecy, in proportion to faith; ministry, in ministering; the teacher, in teaching; the exhorter, in exhortation; the giver, in generosity; the leader, in diligence; the compassionate, in cheerfulness." This list puts leadership second to last, just another important job that needs doing, and characterized particularly by "diligence." "Keep on doing what has to be done." It doesn't sound very high flown. But all together those jobs add up to an exciting enterprise for the church. As Glenn Farquhar-Nicol put it, that enterprise is "about helping others become alive in God—to help people be connected with God and themselves in a new way"—and with others and the world around them.

Don't we need some control? Leaders do need to be assertive. There certainly are ways in which people and churches need to take control over their own lives. Parsons and Leas express appropriate concern about congregations that just don't seem to be able to "get it together," that come up with goals, then can't seem to act on them. The church does need a certain degree of order. In emergencies, such as a nasty church fight in which people just keep tearing each other apart, somebody does need to step in and put an end to vengeful behavior. But to admit that sometimes police action is required is not to say that our values lead us to want to live in a police state. The mothers we talked about earlier would certainly prevent their two-year-olds from running into the street; they would also work toward a time when there was no need for them to exercise that control over their children. You do what's needed in the situation now.

Sometimes clergy get nervous about maintaining control, fearing that lay people will wrest it from them. Under normal circumstances, lay people are not interested in controlling the church, but are concerned about finding power to live their lives in families, communities, and the workplace. Clergy concern about losing control to their parishioners derives more often than not from their own fearful fantasies.

How do we find leaders? The church needs to discover more appropriate ways to discern leadership than the win-lose voting that often ends by reinforcing control on the part of the winners and passivity on the part of the losers. Though Roberts Rules of Order are enshrined as sacred guidelines in many churches, there are other places to look for processes more fitting for a servant church. I hear of Roman Catholic parish councils that are finding some ways of discerning leadership from their heritage. Quakers use "clearness committees" to wait on the Spirit

when faced with decisions. Charles Olsen, a Presbyterian, is studying
how church boards can act as spiritual leaders, not just administrative
groups relying only on secular values and procedures. Discerning new
ways of "corporate spirituality," the boards Olsen is studying find that
"coming to agreement is a work of prayer and of grace."[20]

How do we help people grow toward Integrated authority?

First, Integrated leaders *will* help people grow—just by being who they
are. They will have no interest in keeping others powerless but instead
will be eager to evoke the authority of others and glad to share that
evoking task with many colleagues. Saying clearly who they are and
where they stand, those leaders will encourage others to do the same,
bringing all their experiences and the symbols of the tradition into
enlivening conversation. Their integrative skills will also help people
bring together many dimensions of their inner lives and find connections
between inner life and outer context. Integrated leaders will find creative
ways to join many different people's gifts. They will attend to the process, to "the way we are living together here," to the message conveyed
by the medium. In this they follow One who called himself the Way
(rather than the destination), and made conversations on the road the
centerpiece of his leadership training.

What will these Integrated leaders *do* to help people grow? Here
we have some wisdom from our interviewees who told us which formative experiences had enhanced their own growth in authority.

Several interviewees told stories of being nurtured through *affirmation.* Jim Adams, reflecting on his growing-up years, said, "I've had a
sense that I am a person of worth ever since I was little. (A lot of people
didn't get that kind of gift from their parents.) That authority is now
within me." Verna Dozier also recalled, "My childhood memories are
memories of affirmation... My father...was not educated. But he was
intellectual, cerebral, and I was that way. He was very proud of me. I
came out feeling that my mental processes were worthy." Verna added a
recent story that demonstrated the effects of early affirmation on her
present responses. "I was with a group of clergy... One of the new
clergy there said, 'I don't see how you have the nerve to stand up and
talk to all these clergy!'...I realized that...I have had enough experiences

of affirmation that I'm not afraid to talk to clergy... It never occurred to me that there was anything more remarkable about talking to clergy than talking to lay people."

Reflecting on her experiences of growing up affirmed, Dee Crabtree noted that affirmation makes leaders trustworthy. "Somewhere along the way, I think fairly early in life, I got the message that I was okay...that I could be secure in who I am. I think that the best authority is exerted by those who are secure in who they are... Because if you're insecure you will use authority and power in ways in which you are trying to substitute that for security."

Other interviewees emphasized that their authority had been nurtured by experiences of *challenge*. Joyce Yarrow's early experiences taught her to think for herself and take risks.

> I was an only child. And I was brought up in a family where I could be anything I wanted to be. Gender was not an issue. If I wanted to play baseball, I played baseball. If I wanted to play dolls, I played dolls. I did a lot of son-like things with my father, and a lot of daughter-like things with my mother. I was also challenged by my father at a very young age to think for myself, make decisions for myself, and learn the consequences of my decisions. [My dad] saw potential in me that went well beyond what even I imagined I could do, and he supported me by giving me opportunities to risk a lot, to fail a lot, and to learn by that.

Ruth Shinn's early experiences of challenge implanted in her a "can do" attitude. In college, she wanted to attend a student YWCA conference, but the conference cost $45, and...

> ...there was no money. My parents could give only $2. The Dean of Women said, "The deputation team went out and they turned in some of their collections—We've got $18 for you. Isn't that wonderful?" Well, it was $20 out of $45, and I didn't have anything. So I said, "Do you have a job? I'll work a second job." There was a series of 'No's over a period of weeks, and suddenly, very near the time of the conference, she said, "The college president needs Christmas cards hand addressed. Could you do that?" "Sure!" I went to the conference. It was just overwhelming that what had

been "No!"—just irrevocable boundary—[turned out to be "Yes!" There] was a way out, and ever since then I've been less willing to accept "No" on that kind of basis. I'm ready to say, "Well, is there another way?" And that goes for church budgets and everything else.

Here the balance of support and challenge is strategic. If going to the conference had been easy, Ruth would not remember this story as a marker event on the road to Integrated authority. If she had received less support, she might well have given up in discouragement.

Yarrow and Shinn encountered challenges that formed their basic characters and attitudes. The challenges Judith McMorland and Peter Sherer recall conveyed more specific expectations that "you were there to serve." Judith McMorland, pondering the roots of her authority in an English childhood, reflected,

A lot of it comes out of my family background. We were nurtured for leadership...right from tiny... In relation to the village or the gentry, we were neither, but we were that sort of service professional group in between. There's a very strong social conditioning: this was your lot in life, and you were there to serve on a professional basis. A gradual process of always having been a brownie sixer, a guide leader, a youth leader, a Sunday School teacher, a long, long, slow progression—nothing too desperately stands out. That was the total basis of our family...we were just expected to do what had to be done.

Peter Sherer was challenged to service at home and school.

There are two places that are the sources of my authority. The first is my family, which despite...some parts that I don't consider particularly healthy, gave me a sense very early that I was a Sherer and that we had work to do in the world... That "expected to do things" notion was reinforced in my [school, where the motto was], "Whom to serve is perfect freedom," and the thought was: You who have been especially privileged are especially responsible for using your gifts, so figure out what your gifts are and use them... And so the message was very clear...that I didn't invent these gifts...; they were gifts from God... It was kind of classic noblesse oblige. Those things gave me a sense of myself as a resource...I don't think of myself as some sort of national treasure like the crown jewels or something, but I do feel responsible to use what I've got.

Dorothy McMahon and Colin Bradford told stories about childhood experiences that evoked key qualities—stories in which affirmation and challenge are difficult to distinguish. If pushed, I'd conclude that Dorothy McMahon was *affirmed* into awareness of her gifts. As a child, she recalled,

I was fairly isolated in some ways...and for some reason I became a bit detached from my brothers and sisters. I was also very shy and I used to sit and watch people. And after a while, people used to tell me their life story...I began to be open to the possibility that if people were prepared to trust me with themselves, that maybe there was some...gift that I had...

Colin Bradford's formative experience seems like a paradoxical *challenge* to grow in individuality, on the one hand, and belonging on the other.

I spent a substantial amount of time in two developing countries...I was young so I didn't carry any particular intellectual baggage with me...I put it aside and looked at what was actually going on in the country and...I saw things that other people didn't see.

Anything in your growing up that led you to focus on speaking your voice?

I'm an only child and I spent a lot of time alone...I spent a part of my adolescence on this farm in a God-forsaken place in Western Pennsylvania. And, you know, that experience to some extent created a circumstance of individuality as opposed to a "group person." I'm very group oriented on the other hand, though, maybe in part because of the flip side of that...because of the absence of a stronger and bigger family. So belonging is very important to me.

In Glenn Farquhar-Nicol's childhood experiences, affirmation and challenge seem simply interwoven like a sturdily stitched sampler.

> From a fairly early age people thought I had the gifts to get things done...I can remember at five or six we were expected to make our own beds, do the dishes, take out the garbage. You were told what was right and wrong. The expectations were there. I played all sports. I was the youngest person to be part of the teams. That said something to me about what my capabilities were. There was always a sense of pride in our family... It has to do with homework, for example: the attitude was "Here's an opportunity; make the most of it."

In "good enough" families, affirmation and challenge are not alternatives, but deeply linked. Being received and affirmed naturally flowers into the challenges that press us to Autonomy and Assertion. I am moved by these stories of how people have been nurtured for authority by mothers and fathers like the ones we looked at earlier. When the process of growing and being helped to grow is *working*, as it is for those who tell these stories, what a gentle, loving, and at the same time exciting way to be led into graceful growth in service.

How do we encourage growth in the church?

Churches that aim to be effective servants of our growing up in Christ and our empowerment in ministry can learn from the parents and teachers who nurtured our interviewees toward Integrated authority. First, the message seems clear that our communities of faith must strengthen families so that they can nourish people toward mature authority. Second, our churches can find ways to affirm and challenge their members, doing what's needed at different stages of their development. Let's see what this task might look like as people grow in authority.

Throughout the Receiving stage we can nourish people primarily by affirming them. When we ourselves have let go of control, and are no longer motivated primarily by a need to secure our status and to get people to do what we want them to do, we can affirm children and adults in an open way, finding ways to let each one know, "You are a person of worth." We convey this message in classes and informal conversation by paying attention to people, letting them know their experiences and discoveries are important and worth reflecting on. In classes and other groups, we can create a hospitable climate for the awakening of a core of confidence within each person. Following One who "emptied himself, taking the role of a servant," we will see the teacher as more like a mid-wife than an expert. Instead of rushing in with our answers, we will provide people with opportunities to discover meaning for themselves. We can reflect the insights and wisdom of group members back to them, often in their own words. We will try to be appreciative and patient as people learn the foundational lessons of the Receiving stage—becoming open to God's authority, appreciating and learning from the authority of other members, noticing which models we value and why, learning to take on and carry out a defined task with the support and direction of a mentor or supervisor.

We can continue to provided needed affirmation and challenge as people begin to make the turn toward Autonomy and Assertion. We can nurture young people—not only to accept the authority of their teachers and pastors—but *toward the development of their own authority* as well. Parents and teachers will encourage their offspring and students to respect and challenge authority—including their own. We will all need to be coached toward greater comfort in receiving this challenge.[21] When congregations have discovered that life in the Body requires more than "niceness," they are willing to challenge people. Moving beyond control and passivity means that we can call forth people's initiatives. We will need to watch the balance carefully. Providing affirmation alone yields tame communities that can't confront anybody. Providing challenge alone ends by discouraging people. (Look closely at the beautiful balance Glenn, Joyce, Ruth, and Peter experienced in their families, schools, and churches.) Lifting up the support we experience when we know "we're *together* in this enterprise" and the challenge we meet in recognizing and working with all the *diversity* in our community pro-vides important ways to blend affirmation and challenge.

When I am helped to discern what I have to offer, I am supported and confronted with new possibilities. As servants of our growth, churches send the message Peter Sherer got: "Figure out what your gifts are and use them." Teachers and other leaders can stand ready to help by *noticing*. Perhaps a discerning teacher told Dorothy: "I appreciate your gift for listening deeply to people" —or Colin: "You seem to have a bent toward independent thinking." In Colin's childhood years, a godparent or teacher might usefully have paid attention, not just to an evident talent like his fresh way of perceiving, but also to gifts evoked by some deprivation and consequent longing, noticing how this boy's loneliness and hunger for belonging might issue in passionate support for human communities of all sorts. The empty spaces in our lives may become special openings for God's comfort and call.

The congregation can encourage a "Yes you can!" climate. Our religious community can take it for granted that we will use what we've got. "Go for it!" norms give us courage to risk. Expecting people to do what has to be done is so much more evocative than the all-too-common overfunctioning clergy who are obsessed by their own need to be helpful and compelled to rescue any project that appears to be faltering. Joyce Yarrow's father provided a more useful model of support in giving his daughter chances to fail and learn. So did Glenn's family in telling him, "Here's an opportunity; make the most of it" and standing by supportively while he did just that.[22]

We are unlikely to shift if we haven't been shaken. The evocative community usefully adopts the strategy of *watching the crunch points*. Those times of challenge—times of transition, loss, and crisis—are often important growth points. As a leader with limited time and energy, how wise you will be to watch for those windows of opportunity and provide an extra assist where momentum is already underway.[23] The challenge is a dual one for the leader. When people treat us less than amiably at these anxious junctures, we as leaders require the fortitude not to collapse and let people off the hook because we can't stand it if they aren't nice to us. At the same time, the empowering community needs to provide a safe place in which the crunch and challenge, the shift and shaking, can be borne. It is the leaders' task to help bring into being a strong, caring community that supports people while they surface their anxiety and embarrassment, their terror and despair. We must make it safe enough to look at our fear, hopeful enough to look at our despair, trustworthy enough to look at our anxiety, promising enough to look at the cost.

Churches can continue to support and challenge Assertive folk toward Integrated authority, remembering that the task at this stage is different than it was for people growing in Received authority. Watch the tendency of Receiving and Assertive people to fuse in a stuck symbiosis.

Sensitive leaders will affirm both typically masculine strengths of boldness and initiative and the more typically feminine gift of Receiving and
openness, knowing that "you didn't invent these gifts." Responsible use
of gifts in community is the point, not regarding oneself as a "national
treasure." Perhaps people working on Assertive authority need most to
belong to a community that has moved beyond control and ranking in its
own life. The task is to help people feel secure enough that they aren't
tempted to grab hold of an illusion of security by controlling others.

Throughout all stages of growth, it's important to say "Yes" to
people, to affirm that "What you are emphasizing now is an important
part of the whole picture" rather than putting down Receiving or Assertion because they are partial answers, to accept where people are now
and encourage them to aim their present unfolding toward future wholeness. It's "a long, slow progression," as Judith McMorland acknowledged.

We can live with people in the tension over time. When people
have lived into one pole pretty thoroughly, we can challenge them to
explore the benefits of the other side of that tension. Recall Howard
Ashby's movement from Received to Autonomous authority and Glenn
Farquhar-Nicol's growth from Assertion to Integration. These are not
just movements from one pole of the tension to another; living in the
tension moves us *deeper* as the years go by.

Noticing how people may grow to Integrated authority in the church
has some important implications, of course, for training those who aspire
to lead them in that process. Here are just a few suggestions. When
training leaders, don't lead alone if you can help it. Provide opportunities for others to get the support, affirmation, and challenge of being your
partner. Because people grow in authority in so many different ways and
through so many different stages, it's important, in learning events, to
use lots of different methods—and to be quite comfortable with the
reality that nobody will like all of them! Try to model as many components of Integrated authority as you can, paying special attention to
moments when your less developed strengths are being called for. And
(this is hard) be prepared to process with learners where you failed to do
what the situation required. If you're stretching, you will sometimes fail.
But our failures become useful when we can learn from them. And we
don't have to be perfect. (Peter Sherer's family didn't have to be perfect
to teach him to figure out what his gifts were and use them.) This kind

of openness will help model a norm for a *community* that is always growing.

Situational Leadership: A tool to help servant leaders do what's needed

Can you adapt your leadership style to the needs of the situation and the people with whom you are working? Paul Hersey and Kenneth Blanchard have given us a way to think about what kind of leadership various individuals and groups need under different circumstances and a questionnaire to help us find out how adaptable we are as leaders.

Some of what we do as leaders aims to help people perform the *task*. Leaders also know the *people* themselves are important, and so they pay attention to the effect of their *relationship* on the learners' development. Leaders may be more or less *active* in telling people how to do the task or in the way they relate with those they aim to lead. The learners need more or less help from leaders depending on their stage of development. Beginners might need a lot of instructions on how to do the job and also some support and encouragement as they begin to master it. As learning progresses, the leader will appropriately provide more support ("You can do it!"), continuing to explain and clarify how to do the job but also inviting more participation. As the learners become even more proficient, the leader will continue to provide a lot of support and encouragement but shift toward a more collaborative relationship with the learners, challenging them to take more initiative. Finally, the leader might delegate the job to the now-confident learners and let them get on with it: "I think you can do it now. Take over and keep me posted. Let me know if you need any advice." The leader has enough confidence in the former students to turn the work over to them and direct attention to other matters.[24]

You can assess your own ability to adapt your leadership style to the needs of the situation before you by taking an instrument called "Power Perception Profile," available from the Center for Leadership Studies.[25] Answering the questions may help you assess your situational leadership skills and find out which leadership situations you handle more and less effectively.

Summary

Integrated leadership is evoked by the Body, and it builds the Body. People in our churches are blessed when they have leaders who are intentional about Receiving authority, with its openness to God and other members; Autonomous authority, with its discerning courage; Assertive authority, where energy and boldness become an invitation to the whole community. And we are blessed by leaders who have grown into Integrated strengths like those we have been describing: clarity that authority belongs to God and is delegated by God, a willingness to live with tension and paradox, a perspective that transcends the in-group, a passion for the freedom of others, the evoking of their authority by doing what's needed now. Such leaders can look back with Peter Sherer and say, "I brought the ball, and I don't have to be the captain," and they can affirm with Dee Crabtree, "The only way we can equip the saints is to honor them as saints. And that's what my kind of authority tries to do."

Let's take a last look at how some of those strengths shine forth in a most ordinary story about a woman who was asked to chair a committee. Judith McMorland, laywoman from Auckland, tells about

> the work we did in the diocese, when we were looking at the diocese in review... There were a committee of eight and I'd been asked by the bishop to be on that committee because I'd been very rude about the clergy anyhow, and had made a lot of noises and also came out of that management sort of background so the thought was 'she can get on with it.' Working particularly with Peter Beck, we claimed within the group to do it differently. The very first meeting we had, somehow the eight people caught it and thereafter all the process things we did, which were claiming the authority to be the guardians of the process—it all flowed wonderfully. Everybody was fully there on their own authority. There wasn't any sense of not being peers, but we had different skills. The immediate image is of a golden rain firework. Ah! Just sort of gentle, and lots of sparks, sparkles. Not rockets, just a little gentle rain.

For your reflection, envisioning, and discernment of your next steps

How can you, too, with your unique gifts, in the places where you find yourself, begin to bring to birth the vision for the church toward which you are called by God, in a willing, not a willful way? You might use the following reflection process to guide you toward finding your own answers to that question. This process could easily be adapted for a day's retreat for a group.

1. Images and metaphors for the church spark vision. It may be helpful to begin with a metaphor that seems to you to hold possibilities for inspiring a vision for the church. Perhaps those we have discussed in this chapter: a colony of heaven, or the Body of Christ, or the church as Servant. Or substitute another metaphor that seems right to you.[26]
What kind of vision does your metaphor open up? What cherished values for the church does it point toward?

2. What are the things you value or deplore most about the church as you EXPERIENCE it? Where is it most transparent for God? Where is it radiant with energy and life? Where do you experience the church offering itself in a transforming way for the world?
In what ways do you see the church most dead, most lacking in energy and transparency for God, most controlling or passive?

3. Expand your vision beyond the purely linear and rational level. Describe your vision for the church that begins to emerge out of your mulling over the questions above. Find an open way to play with this vision. You might take colors and paper and see what comes, or write a story about that church. You might think of music or biblical symbols that express the true nature of that church. Or write a dialogue with that church. Keep grounding your vision in your own experience, remembering times and places when you have encountered that reality in the church you know.

4. Now think about what you have to offer. What gifts do you bring to your role in the church? Where are you in your own development in authority at this time, and what does that suggest about what you have to contribute? What ways seem to be open to you now to make a difference—to support more transparency, energy, and abundant life in the church?

5. What about others with whom you share responsibility? Where do they seem to be? Do you see ways of evoking their authority and encouraging them on the way? Recall any interviewees' stories about how they were nurtured for authority that struck you on first reading. Is there anybody you collaborate with, supervise, or teach with whom you're in a position to provide affirmation or suggest a challenge?
What kind of leadership seems to be needed in the situations that concern you right now? (Review your answers to the Situational Leadership Survey, if you took it.)

6. Pulling it all together: your sense of calling in the church. What thoughts so far seem most compelling? Where do you feel deeply drawn? What do you seem called to do now to support present strengths and help your vision for the church become a reality? Spend some time praying about that, then writing about it, and, finally, summarize what you have written with a title.

7. What are some of the barriers to your doing those things? List those you can think of. How might you counter those barriers in useful ways? How can you ally yourself with forces that are supporting graced present realities or useful change?

8. What are the first steps? What is the first step?

9. Who is a partner, or who might be a group of people, who will help hold you accountable for what you have undertaken to do?

10. When will you undertake to review your intention in prayer and with your partner or group and revise it in the light of changing events and understandings? One month? Six months? A year? Make an entry in your calendar.

The Research Study

List of Interviewees

The Rev. James R. Adams
Rector, St. Mark's Church
Capitol Hill
Washington, DC
Date of birth: June 30, 1934
ISTJ

The Rev. Susan Adams
At the time of the interview: Parish Vicar
Presently Diocesan Coordinator of Ministry Education
Anglican Diocese of Auckland, N.Z.
Date of birth: July 20, 1947
ENTJ

The Rev. Howard Ashby
Parish Vicar, Prison Chaplain
Tongariro Prison Farm
Turangi, N.Z.
Anglican
Date of birth: February 5, 1942

The Rev. Loma Balfour
Vicar, Parish of Rangiora
N.Z.
Anglican
Date of birth: February 2, 1940
ENFJ

Colin Bradford
Economist
At the time of the interview on the staff of the World Bank
Presently Director of Research, OECD
Paris
Episcopal
Date of birth: 1939
ENFP

The Rev. Davida Foy Crabtree
At the time of the interview: Senior Minister
Colchester Federated Church
Colchester, CT
Presently, Conference Minister, Southern California Conference, UCC
Date of birth: June 7, 1944
ENFP

Verna J. Dozier
Retired teacher, public schools
Washington, DC
Free lance consultant in Bible study and the ministry of the laity
Author of *Authority of the Laity*
Episcopal
Date of birth: October 9, 1917
INFJ

The Rev. Glenn Farquhar-Nicol
Minister, Glebe Parish
Sydney, Australia
Uniting Church in Australia
Date of birth: January 24, 1957
ENFJ

The Rev. Dwight Lundgren
Senior Minister, First Baptist Church
Providence, RI
American Baptist
Date of birth: June 20, 1944
ENTJ

Keith Mason, Q.C.
Solicitor General, New South Wales
Sydney, Australia
Anglican
Date of birth: February 18, 1947
IXTJ

The Rev. Dorothy McMahon
Minister, Pitt Street Uniting Church
Sydney, Australia
Date of Birth: April 7, 1934
ENFP

Dr. Judith McMorland
Teacher of personnel management, industrial training,
and organizational change, University of Auckland,
Centre for Continuing Education
N.Z.
Anglican
Date of birth: May 29, 1942
ENTJ

Peter Sherer
Senior Development Officer
National Community AIDS Partnership
Washington, DC
Alexandria, VA
Episcopal
Date of birth: May 23, 1946
ENFP

Ruth Shinn
Chief of the Division of Legislative Analysis
Women's Bureau
U.S. Department of Labor
Washington, DC
United Church of Christ
ENFP

Richard Tustian
Retired, Land Use Planner
Bethesda, MD
Presbyterian

Joyce Yarrow
President, Institute for Nonprofit Training and Development, Inc.
Hartford, CT
United Church of Christ
Date of birth: April 15, 1942
ENFP

The Interview Questions

1. *What is authority for you*, in your experience?

2. (Three questions on *leadership style*): Do you tend to focus on the task more or to support the people you're working with more? Do you more often try to help the group say what they think or do you say what you think right away? Do you know what your MBTI type is?

3. *Where do you get your authority*, do you think? (Probe for *experienced* sources.) People sometimes think of the source of their authority as *within themselves*, or *granted by the people they work with*, or as *coming from God*. Or they may say all of those are true. Or they may want to put it another way. What would you say? Were there any *experiences* that were particularly important in your developing a sense of your own authority?

I'd like to explore with you the difficulties you find exercising your authority and also the strengths you show and the joy you may find. Let's start with some of the difficulties.

4. *Caught between vision and people.*
People sometimes find themselves caught between their wish to put forward a vision and their concern not to alienate people. To push for something you know is important—or to hold back to keep from being pushy. Do you ever get caught that way? How do you work with that conflict?

5. *When your authority was challenged.*
Think of a time when your authority was challenged. What happened? What was the nature of the crunch for you? What sustains you at a time like that?

6. *Authority and role*
Let's look at what your role has to do with your authority. Is your authority very dependent on a role? Or quite independent of a role? Or somewhere in between? People sometimes find themselves in a place where the exercise of their authority seems almost to run the risk of crushing someone else. (Sometimes this crunch results from the heavy demands of a person's role in an institution.) How do you tend to respond when you find yourself in that bind?

7. *Graceful authority*
Think of a graceful moment when you could say, "Yes, this is what my authority is for." A time when you really felt strong and clear in your authority. What was that time like? Can you think of an image or a metaphor that captures it? What *is* the purpose of your authority?

8. *Projections*
What do you do when people project their authority onto you, when they attribute to you more than is yours, and you feel it must be "their stuff"? Have you learned any helpful ways to respond to people who do that? How do you live appropriately with excessive admiration, when it comes your way?

9. *Male or Female*

Do you find any special strength or difficulty in dealing with your authority because you are a woman/man? (Probes if needed: Some women report difficulty in operating out of their own center. Has that ever been true for you? Some men report difficulty in separating authority and domination. Has that ever been true for you?) In exercising authority, some people would see themselves primarily as "set over" other people, others would say they are primarily "set apart" or "set alongside." Which seems truest for you?

10. *Ordained or lay*

What's special about your authority as an ordained/lay person? Where is the most impoortant arena for your authority? What are the unique requirements of that arena?

11. *Last thoughts /Biblical references*

Any last thoughts? Any stories or passages in the Bible that remind you of what you've said about your authority?

Acknowledgments

I was fortunate to have as my tutor in Australia Dorothy Lee-Pollard, New Testament Instructor at United Theological College near Sydney, and in New Zealand, Francis Foulkes, Warden and Professor of New Testament at The College of St. John the Evangelist. They guided my word studies on *exousia* (authority) and my efforts to discern the picture of Jesus' authority in the gospel stories. Dorothy Lee, now Professor of New Testament at Theological Hall, Synod of Victoria, in Melbourne, kindly read and critiqued several sections of the manuscript which drew on our NT studies. Jackson Carroll, then of Hartford Seminary and presently at Duke University Divinity School, made especially helpful suggestions for the bibliography. Douglas A. Walrath, Barbara Gilbert, and Loren B. Mead kindly reviewed the interview questions and made helpful suggestions for improving them. Terry Foland, as member of the Alban Research Committee, reviewed the entire manuscript.

NOTES

Chapter 1

1. Kittel, *Theological Dictionary of the New Testament* (Grand Rapids: Eerdman, 1985).

2. *The Washington Post*, 2/11/90, A28.

Chapter 2

1. See, for example, the work of Erikson, Loevinger, Kohlberg, Belenky, Westerhoff, and Fowler.

2. David McClelland, *Power: The Inner Experience* (New York: Irvington, 1975).

3. John C. Harris, *Stress, Power, and Ministry* (Washington, DC: The Alban Institute, 1977).

4. Cf. McClelland, op. cit., ll7.

5. Harris, op. cit., 110.

6. Ibid., 111.

7. Mary Field Belenky, Blyth McVicker Clinchy, Nancy Rule Goldberger, Jill Mattuck Tanele, *Women's Way of Knowing* (New York: Basic Books, 1986), 175.

8. Edwin Friedman, *Generation to Generation: Family Process in Church and Synagogue* (New York: Guilford Press, 1985).

9. Richard Sennett, *Authority* (New York: Alfred A. Knopf, 1980), 180.

10. Ibid., 87-88.

11. Barry Evans, "Clergy and Their Parishes," *Action Information* (Sept.-Oct. 1989).

12. Paul Tillich, *Love, Power, & Justice* (New York and London: Oxford University Press, 1954), 36.

13. Ken Kesey, *One Flew Over the Cuckoo's Nest* (New York: A Signet Book, New American Library, 1962).

14. Op. cit., 194.

15. *The Washington Post,* Jan. 1, 1991, 1.

16. Werner H. Kelber, *Mark's Story of Jesus* (Philadelphia: Fortress, 1979), 72-3.

17. E. Schweizer, *The Good News According to Mark* (London: SPCK, 1971), 313.

18. Sennett, op. cit., 22.

19. Jim Adams, *Action Information* (February 1975).

20. Davida Crabtree, *The Empowering Church* (Washington, DC: The Alban Institute, 1989).

21. John Howard Yoder, *The Fullness of Christ: Paul's Vision of Universal Ministry* (Elgin, IL: Brethren Press, 1987), 17.

22. Walter Wink, *Naming the Powers: the language of power in the New Testament* (Philadelphia: Fortress Press, 1984), 146.

23. Yoder, op. cit., 67.

24. Barbara Gilbert, *Who Ministers to Ministers* (Washington, DC: The Alban Institute, 1987), 42.

25. Harris, op. cit., 54.

26. Collected Works, Vol. II, tr. by R.F.C. Hull (Princeton University Press, 1969), 339, qt. in E. M. Prevallet, S.L. "Through an Autumn Lens," *Weavings* (May/June 1991, Vol. VI, no. 3).

27. D. E. Nineham, *Saint Mark,* (Penguin, 1963), 439.

28. John C. Fletcher, *Religious Authenticity in the Clergy* (Washington, DC: The Alban Institute, 1975).

29. Raymond E. Brown, *The Gospel According to John,* The Anchor Bible (Garden City, New York: Doubleday & Co., 1966), 1016.

30. Ibid.

31. Janet Morley, *All Desires Known* (Auckland, NZ: *Women's Resource Centre,* 1988), 14.

Chapter 3

1. Harris, op. cit., 69.

2. Jackson W. Carroll, *As One With Authority, Reflective*

Leadership in Ministry (Louisville: Westminster/John Knox Press, 1991), 199.

    3. Op. cit., 67.

    4. Sennett, op. cit., 33.

    5. Ibid., 129.

    6. Wink, op. cit., 146.

Chapter 4

    1. McClelland, op. cit., 121.

    2. Belenky et al., op. cit., 134.

    3. Belenky et al., op. cit., 209.

    4. Polly Young-Eisendrath and Florence Wiedeman, *Female Authority* (New York: Guilford Press, 1987), 49.

    5. Young-Eisendrath and Wiedeman, op. cit., 125.

    6. Ibid., 59.

    7. See Celia Hahn, *Sexual Paradox,* (New York: Pilgrim Press, 1991) Chapter 2 for a fuller discussion of these dynamics.

    8. Young-Eisendrath and Wiedeman, op. cit., 43.

    9. Ibid., 47, 44.

    10. Belenky et al., op. cit., 17-18.

    11. Carol Pierce, with Bill Page, *A Male/Female Continuum: Paths to Colleagueship* (Laconia, NH: New Dynamics, 1986), 18.

    12. Cynthia Fuchs Epstein, et al., "Ways Men and Women Lead," *Harvard Business Review* (January-February 1991, p. 150-160), 158.

    13. McClelland, op. cit., 186.

    14. Ibid.

    15. McClelland, op. cit., 61.

    16. e.g., Daniel Levinson.

    17. McClelland, op. cit., 209-10.

    18. McClelland, op. cit., 212.

    19. In this section I am indebted to the work of Carol Pierce.

    20. McClelland, op. cit., 152.

    21. Belenky, et al., op. cit., 135.

    22. Ibid.

    23. Ibid.

    24. Young-Eisendrath and Wiedeman, op. cit., 64.

25. Lynn M. Rhodes, *Co-Creating: A Feminist Vision of Ministry* (Westminster, 1987), 47.

26. Belenky et al., op. cit., 137.

27. Young-Eisendrath and Wiedeman, op. cit., 141.

Chapter 5

1. James R. Adams and Celia A. Hahn, "Ministry in the Church; Ministry in the World—What's the Connection?" *Action Information* (July-August, 1986). This section draws on the argument in that article.

2. Edwin H. Friedman, Video: *Family Process and Process Theology.* (Washington, DC: The Alban Institute, 1991).

3. Fletcher, op. cit.

Chapter 6

1. Friedman, op. cit., 218.

2. Maggie Ross, *Pillars of Flame: Power, Priesthood, and Spiritual Maturity* (San Francisco: Harper & Row, 1988), 54.

3. Sennett, op. cit., 156.

4. c.f. Belenky et al, op. cit., 18, 96, 416.

5. Harris, op. cit., 36-7.

6. Ibid., 40.

7. I have been much helped by the work of Paul Stevens and Phil Collins in *The Equipping Pastor* (Washington, DC: The Alban Institute, 1993), especially in their joining of systems theory and the Body of Christ.

8. Nancy Myer Hopkins, "Symbolic Church Fights," *Congregations* (May-June, 1993).

9. Stevens and Collins, op. cit.

10. Here I want to acknowledge a debt to Friedman, op. cit., though I have reframed the discussion.

11. Translated by Coleman Barks with John Moyne. Rick and Louise Nelson, *Written in the Language of the Heart*, p. 90, copyright the authors, 1993.

12. Arlin J. Rothauge, *Sizing Up a Congregation* (New York: Episcopal Church Center).

13. Sennett, op. cit., 167.

14. Ibid.

15. Ibid., 163.

16. Loren B. Mead makes this helpful point.

17. This thinking comes from *Ministry in America*, David S. Schuller, Merton P. Strommen, and Milo Brekke, editors. An exhaustive study of ministry in the U.S. and Canada. (San Francisco: Harper & Row, 1980).

18. Ross, op. cit., 51.

19. George Parsons and Speed Leas, *Understanding Your Congregation as a System* [Manual] (Washington, DC: The Alban Institute, 1993), 35.

20. Charles Olsen, "What Makes Church Boards Work," *Congregations*, (May-June, July-August 1993).

21. See Parsons and Leas, op. cit. for specific suggestions from Speed Leas.

22. For specific designs for gift discernment, see *What Do I Have To Offer?* by Hahn, Adams, Amy, and Lloyd—an Alban Institute On Demand Publication.

23. Helpfully stressed by Loren B. Mead.

24. "Situational Leadership: A Summary," developed by Paul Hersey (Center for Leadership Studies, 230 W 3rd Ave., Escondido, CA 92025, copyright 1976 by Leadership Studies, Inc).

25. Power Perception Profile (Center for Leadership Studies, 230 W 3rd Ave., Escondido, CA 92025). Single copies are $2.95, quantity orders less.

26. See Keith Russell, *In Search of the Church* (Washington, DC: The Alban Institute, 1994), for several suggestions.

BIBLIOGRAPHY

Achtemeier, Paul J. *Mark.* Philadelphia: Fortress Press, 1986.

Bauer. *Encyclopedia of Biblical Theology.* Sheed & Ward, 1970.

Belenky, Mary Field; Clinchy, Blyth McVicker; Goldberger, Nancy Rule; Tanele, Jill Mattuck. *Women's Ways of Knowing: The Development of Self, Voice, and Mind.* New York: Basic Books, 1986.

Brown, Raymond E. *The Gospel According to John,* The Anchor Bible. Garden City, New York: Doubleday & Co., 1966.

Carroll, Jackson W. *As One With Authority.* Louisville: Westminster/ John Knox Press, 1991.

Carroll, Jackson W. "Some Issues in Clergy Authority." *Review of Religious Research* Vol. 23, No. 2 (December 1981).

Clifford, Richard J. *Fair Spoken and Persuading: An Interpretation of Second Isaiah.* New York: Paulist Press, 1984.

Crabtree, Davida Foy. *The Empowering Church: How One Congregation Supports Lay People's Ministries in the World.* Washington, DC: The Alban Institute, 1989.

Dominian, Jack. *Authority: A Christian Interpretation of the Psychological Evolution of Authority.* London: Burns & Oates, 1976.

Dozier, Verna J., with Celia A. *The Authority of the Laity* . Washington, DC: The Alban Institute, 1982.

Durka, Gloria. "Women, Power, and the Work of Religious Education," in *Changing Patterns of Religious Education*. Ed. by Marvin J. Taylor. Nashville: Abingdon Press, 1984.

Economist, The. "Women in Management," no byline. London: March 28, 1992, p. 17-20, Vol. 322, No. 7752.

Epstein, Cynthia Fuchs, et al. "Ways Men and Women Lead: Readers and Authors Face Off Over HBR's Last Issue." *Harvard Business Review* (January-February 1991): 150-160.

Evans, Barry. "Clergy and Their Parishes." *Action Information* (September-October 1959).

Fletcher, John C. *Religious Authenticity in the Clergy*. Washington, DC: The Alban Institute, 1975.

Freire, Paulo. *Pedagogy of the Oppressed*, Chs. 1-2. New York: Seabury Press, 1970.

Friedman, Edwin H. *Generation to Generation: Family Systems in Church and Synagogue*. New York: Guilford Press, 1985.

Gilbert, Barbara. *Who Ministers to Ministers?* Washington, DC: The Alban Institute, 1987.

Gray, Janette. "Jesus and Women—The Johannine Community Responds," Unpublished paper, 1986, United Theological College, Sydney, Australia.

Greenleaf, Robert K. "The Servant as Leader" in *Servant Leadership: a Journey Into the Nature of Legitimate Power and Greatness*. New York: Paulist Press, 1977.

Hahn, Celia Allison. *Lay Voices in an Open Church*. Washington, DC: The Alban Institute, 1984.

Hahn, Celia Allison. *Sexual Paradox: Creative Tensions in Our Lives and in Our Congregations.* New York: Pilgrim Press, 1991.

Hahn, Celia Allison; Adams, James R.; Amy, Anne Gavin; Lloyd, Barton. *What Do I Have To Offer?* Washington, DC: The Alban Institute, 1978.

Harris, John C. *Stress, Power, and Ministry.* Washington, DC: The Alban Institute, 1977.

Harrison, Paul M. *Authority and Power in the Free Church Tradition.* Princeton, NJ: Princeton University Press, 1959.

Hengel, Martin. *Christ and Power.* Philadelphia: Fortress Press, 1977.

Hersey, Paul. "Situational Leadership: A Summary," Leadership Studies, Inc., 1976.

Hersey and Blanchard. "Power Perception Profile," Center for Leadership Studies, 230 W. 3rd Ave., Escondido, CA 92025.

Holmberg, Bengt. *Paul and Power.* CWK Gleerup, Coniectanea Biblica, New Testament Series, Sweden: Studentlitteratur AB, Lund, 1978.

Ice, Martha Long. *Clergy Women and Their Worldviews: Calling for A New Age.* New York: Praeger, 1987.

The Interpreter's Dictionary of the Bible. Nashville: Abingdon Press, 1962.

Keen, Sam. *The Passionate Life: Stages of Loving.* San Francisco: Harper & Row, 1983.

Kelber, Werner H. *Mark's Story of Jesus.* Philadelphia: Fortress Press, 1979.

Lash, Nicholas. *Voices of Authority.* London: Sheed & Ward, 1976.

MacDonald, Dennis R. *The Legend and the Apostle: The Battle for Paul in Story and Canon.* Philadelphia: Westminster Press, 1983.

McClelland, David C. *Power: The Inner Experience.* New York: Irvington, 1975.

McGinlay, Hugh, Ed. *The Year of Mark.* Northcote, Australia: Desbook and The Joint Board of Christian Education of Australia and New Zealand, 1987.

McMahon, Dorothy. "Power and Authority in the Christian Church," *Ministry.* Board of Education, Uniting Church in Australia, New South Wales Synod, P.O. Box E 178, St. James NSW 2000 Australia.

Morrison, Clinton. *An Analytical Concordance to the Revised Standard Version of the New Testament.* Philadelphia: Westminster Press, 1979.

Nineham, D. E. *Saint Mark.* Penguin Books, 1963.

Palmer, Parker. *Leading From Within: Reflections on Spirituality and Leadership.* Indianapolis, IN: Indiana Office for Campus Ministries, 1990.

Parsons, George, and Leas, Speed. *Understanding Your Congregation As a System,* Manual. Washington, DC: The Alban Institute, 1994.

Pierce, Carol, with Page, Bill. *A Male/Female Continuum: Paths to Colleagueship.* Laconia, NH: New Dynamics, 1986.

Reed, Bruce D. *The Dynamics of Religion: Process and Movement in Christian Churches.* London: Darton, Longman & Todd, 1978.

Rhodes, Lynn N. *Co-Creating: A Feminist Vision of Ministry.* Philadelphia: Westminster Press, 1987.

Richardson, Alan and John Bowden. *A New Dictionary of Christian Theology.* SCM Press, 1983.

Rosener, Judy B. "Ways Women Lead." *Harvard Business Review* (November-December 1990): 119-125.

Ross, Maggie. *Pillar of Flame: Power, Priesthood, and Spiritual Maturity*. San Francisco: Harper & Row, 1988.

Russell, Anthony. *The Clerical Profession*. London: SPCK, 1980.

Russell, Letty M. *The Future of Partnership*. Philadelphia: Westminster Press, 1979.

Schaef, Anne Wilson. "Is the Church an Addictive Organization?" *The Christian Century* (January 3-10, 1990, Vol. 107, No. 1): 18-21.

Schneiders, Sandra. "The Footwashing (John 13:1-20): An Experiment in Hermeneutics," *Ex Auditu*. (Vol. I, 1985) Princeton Theological Seminary.

Sennett, Richard. *Authority*. New York: Alfred A. Knopf, 1980.

Steele, David A. *Images of Leadership and Authority For the Church*. Lanham, MD: University Press of America

Stevens, Paul, and Collins, Phil. *The Equipping Pastor*. Washington, DC: The Alban Institute, 1993

Suchocki, Marjorie Hewitt. "Friends in the Family: Church, Seminary, and Theological Education," in *Beyond Clericalism*. Ed. by Joseph C. Hough, Jr. and Barbara G. Wheeler. Atlanta: Scholars Press, 1988.

Tillich, Paul. *Love, Power, and Justice*. New York and London: Oxford University Press, 1954.

Underhill, Evelyn. *The Life of the Spirit and the Life of Today*. New York: Harper & Row, 1986.

Walker, Barbara G. *The Crone*. San Francisco: Harper & Row, 1985.

Wink, Walter. *Naming the Powers: the Language of Power in the New Testament.* Philadelphia: Fortress Press, 1984.

Yoder, John Howard. *The Fullness of Christ: Paul's Vision of Universal Ministry.* Elgin, IL: Brethren Press, 1987.

Young-Eisendrath, Polly and Wiedeman, Florence. *Female Authority: Empowering Women Through Psychotherapy.* New York: Guilford Press, 1987.

The Alban Institute:
an invitation to membership

The Alban Institute, begun in 1979, believes that the congregation is essential to the task of equipping the people of God to minister in the church and the world. A multi-denominational membership organization, the Institute provides on-site training, educational programs, consulting, research, and publishing for hundreds of churches across the country.

The Alban Institute invites you to be a member of this partnership of laity, clergy, and executives—a partnership that brings together people who are raising important questions about congregational life and people who are trying new solutions, making new discoveries, finding a new way of getting clear about the task of ministry. The Institute exists to provide you with the kinds of information and resources you need to support your ministries.

Join us now and enjoy these benefits:

CONGREGATIONS, The Alban Journal, a highly respected journal published six times a year, to keep you up to date on current issues and trends.

Inside Information, Alban's quarterly newsletter, keeps you informed about research and other happenings around Alban. Available to members only.

Publications Discounts:

☐ 15% for Individual, Retired Clergy, and Seminarian Members
☐ 25% for Congregational Members
☐ 40% for Judicatory and Seminary Executive Members

Discounts on Training and Education Events

Write our Membership Department at the address below or call us at 1-800-486-1318 or 301-718-4407 for more information about how to join The Alban Institute's growing membership, particularly about Congregational Membership in which 12 designated persons receive all benefits of membership.

The Alban Institute, Inc.
Suite 433 North
4550 Montgomery Avenue
Bethesda, MD 20814-3341

262.1
H148

LINCOLN CHRISTIAN COLLEGE AND SEMINARY   88520

262.1 H148   88520
Hahn, Celia A.
Growing in authority,
 relinquishing control

DEMCO